GW01260439

Heroes Pub

MOODY BLUES
following the second best team in Europe

James Clarke

First published in Great Britain in 2008 by
Heroes Publishing.
P.O. Box 1703, Perry Barr,
Birmingham B42 1UZ.

ISBN 0-9543884-9-6

–

EAN 97809543884-9-2

Cover design by www.nineteen76-designs.co.uk

Printed by Thomson Litho

Acknowledgements

Thanks to everyone who makes matchdays so enjoyable – John, Margaret, Dan, Mark, Chris, John, Tim, Tony, Big Sam and anyone I've forgotten.

Thanks to Dave for making this book happen and to Simon for pointing me in his direction to begin with and helping me keep matchdays free.

Thanks to my family for all their support and particularly to Dad for introducing me to Chelsea in the first place. What might have happened if you hadn't?

Thanks to the old bloke selling fanzines, who calls them the *"new official book of Chelsea"*, for always bringing a smile to my face.

Thanks to National Express for getting me up and down the M40 so cheaply – I spend almost as many hours asleep in your coaches as I do in my own bed.

Oh and thanks to Chelsea for being the best football team in the world – even if not always the best football club.

This book is for Ken Clarke and Steve Harris, neither of whom lived to see as many Chelsea matches as they should have done.

James Clarke,
Summer 2008.

Contents

Introduction

I'm a Chelsea fan. Sorry.

These are words I've found myself saying a lot in recent years. If you say you're a Chelsea fan people assume you started liking football in 2003, you wouldn't know a Wednesday night in Grimsby if it slapped you round the face and you've never heard of Doug Rougvie or Dale Jasper.

I have. Some of us have been around since before Abramovich took over. I have one brilliant get-out clause when accused of being a gloryhunter. The season I started supporting Chelsea was our worst ever. 1982-83, when an end-of-season Clive Walker winner at Bolton avoided relegation to division three. We finished 18th. I was seven. And hooked.

I'm a third generation fan. My grandfather adopted Chelsea as his team when he moved to London from Scotland between the wars, my dad and uncle Ken followed in his footsteps and I've done the same. I grew up in East London and there were no other Chelsea fans at my school. I spent years explaining how I could support such a rubbish team. This decade I've spent years explaining how I could support such a successful team. That's football.

We moved to Sussex when I was 12, meaning I had to keep in touch from afar as a teenager with posters of Andy Townsend, Graham Stuart and Paul Elliott on the wall. I began to go regularly in the mid-nineties in my late teens and got my first season ticket as soon as I could afford one, four years ago. It arrived in the post the morning after Abramovich's takeover was announced. Immaculate timing – I had a season ticket as the amazing new dawn began and could also prove I'd ordered it before knowing we were about to become rich.

I now live in Birmingham. I moved up here from Hastings two years ago for work. When I accepted the new job so many people asked me "What about going to Chelsea?" I was bemused. It never even crossed my mind to stop going. I travel down from Birmingham to London and the thought of not going is alien.

What else can I tell you? Like many Chelsea fans of my sort of age my childhood hero was Kerry Dixon, I idolised Gianfranco Zola and my favourite current player is Frank Lampard. But I have Joe Cole's name and number on the back of my shirt. I lost patience with Shaun Wright-Phillips last season, wish we hadn't sold Arjen Robben and Eidur Gudjohnsen and think it's a great shame they've banned celery. I always walk up the left-hand side of the stairs at Fulham Broadway Tube station and it's more than a decade since I last went to a game not wearing blue pants.

I'm a Chelsea fan. Welcome to my world.

Chapter 1

Back to the Bridge

Sunday August 5
Manchester United (Wembley)

Last season ended with a match against Manchester United at Wembley, this season starts with a match against Manchester United at Wembley. Who says modern football is boring and repetitive? But while I'm aware that football is becoming dominated by the elite few, I won't be grumbling if I end the day as happy as I ended FA Cup final day three months ago.

Living in Birmingham means a 200-ish mile round trip for home games, and for trips to Wembley. I normally travel down by National Express coach. It goes to Victoria, which is walking distance from Chelsea, and can be as little as a quid each way. Yes, I know that's ridiculously cheap, and it's why I put myself through the trauma of a two hour and 50 minute ride on a hot and crowded coach, sitting unpleasantly close to a complete stranger, twice in a day every other weekend.

But today it's the train. The Chiltern route from Birmingham to London features a stop at Wembley Stadium station – right next to the ground, so it makes sense to come this way. The journey down sees me surrounded by United fans, some heading down from Manchester, others from the Midlands. Bloody gloryhunters. They get everywhere.

It's so hot and sunny I soon realise I'm going to get sunburnt (I am 'pale and interesting' and could get burnt just reading the Sun). So I nip into the Wembley branch of Lidl for some factor 15 sun cream. First game of the season and the first ludicrously un-football-fan-like activity.

I'm down low behind the goal. Shortly before kick-off I get a call on my mobile from Mark, who sits two seats along from me at the Bridge. He asks where I am and when I describe my location he realises I'm about 15 yards away and wanders over for a chat. It's good to see him. Having a season ticket can mean you sit next to people every game for nine months at a time then go three months without seeing them, with only the occasional text or email about an exciting new signing to tide you over.

We discuss new boys Malouda, Pizarro, Ben-Haim and Sidwell (good, quite good, okay and not sure), the departure of Robben (bad) and the fact that Jose seems to have forgotten to pick any strikers today. Looking at the players we have starting the game, we seem to have three wingers but no striker. Is this a new-found 4-6-0 formation?

As the game starts it emerges that Joe Cole is our striker. Wonderful winger, wonderful midfielder, not a centre forward. United are well on top and take the lead through Giggs. It's fully deserved. But just before the break Malouda, who has been our best player, equalises.

Malouda looks good. If he's going to replace Robben he'll have to be. In the second half he's replaced by Pizarro, who looks a bit unfit, so much so you'd probably not play him even if he was your only available forward. Mystery solved.

There are no more goals in the second half, so it's penalties. It seems ridiculous to decide the Charity Shield like this. They used to share it if it was a draw and I can't see why they don't now. It's a glorified friendly, if it ends up a draw so be it. Of course my attitude has nothing to do with the fact we can't do penalty shoot-outs. Some of my fellow fans are leaving before the shoot-out even starts, so confident are they in our ability. And they're soon proved right. Van Der Sar saves three out of three from Pizarro, Lampard and Wright-Phillips, while United score all of theirs. Good job it's only the Charity Shield eh? Who wants to win a big plate?

Sunday August 12
Birmingham (home)

I may have had the trip to Wembley last week, but this is the real start of the season. First league game, first trip to the Bridge. This is where the season really begins.

The opening home match is always special. New players to see, a return to your second home and the chance to see some old friends. When you get a season ticket you're in the lap of the Gods as to who you end up surrounded by. You could be next to someone really boring, in front of a shouter or near a load of arseholes. But I'm lucky enough to have been placed with some smashing people. They are, as follows:

John and Margaret, a lovely couple who travel from Cornwall for every home game, having moved there when they retired. You can't help but admire their commitment. They're delightful people. John was at Stamford Bridge when we won the league in 1955 and I've been really pleased for him being able to see the second and third titles five decades on. Margaret's been coming with him almost as long. She worries about the team and finds it impossible to watch if we have a penalty or some such other moment of high drama.

Dan, a good bloke in his twenties who travels from Surrey and always misses at least the first two minutes of the game because he's lingered too long in the pub. He also goes off for a pint at half-time and therefore misses the first five minutes of most second halves. He should try to get a partial refund on his season ticket.

Mark, who I saw at Wembley last week. Another nice bloke, he's a fitness trainer and used to work with Joe Cole's missus. He's pretty mild-mannered but manages to get into at least one big argument a season, normally when someone three rows back has slagged off one of his favourite players.

Dan's drinking buddies **Chris and John**, a father and son. Chris has a booming voice, utilised best when shouting "BISON!!!!" whenever Michael Essien makes a storming run up the pitch. John, a medical student, slags off the referee in every game, convinced there's an anti-Chelsea conspiracy among them. Also in the row behind are **Tim and Tony**, who are always willing to join Mark and I in laughing at Dan for turning up for a game in a fluorescent pink or orange Adidas track top, which he's prone to do.

Big Sam. He has no idea who we are but we know all about him. Mark and Dan christened him Sam long before I sat there. Sits a couple of rows in front of us and a few seats to the left. A big man, he has the world's most expressive hands. These are used to indicate time-wasting by the opposition, through point-ing at his watch, but they also conjure up hundreds of other sig-nals each game. Dan, Mark and I have spent hours of our lives watching him in action over the years. We often speculate as to whether he has a manicure as a pre-match preparation, how much his precious watch cost or whether he has special gloves to keep his hands fresh for action. We've watched him eat pies, discussed what he might do for a living, wondered where he lives, hoped there's a Mrs Sam and have even contemplated fol-lowing him home. Dan once asked someone who sits near him what his name was and we were disappointed to find it wasn't Sam. But we've carried on calling him Big Sam. I took a sneaky photo of him in a pub in Barcelona to text back to Dan and Mark when I spotted him out there. You could say we're stalking him.

As well as meeting up with my friends there's a game today. Birmingham have just come back up and we should beat them. So of course Birmingham take the lead. Forssell, our old boy, gets the goal. Pizarro equalises three minutes later, Malouda puts us in front, but Kapo equalises for them. Four goals by half-time! There's only one in the second half, a winner for us from Essien.

Two goals from new boys and a five goal thriller with attack-ing football, quality and mistakes from both teams. As we leave the ground we all talk about how much we've enjoyed this new attacking Chelsea. All except Big Sam that is. He talks to his own friends, because he has no idea who we are.

Wednesday August 15
Reading (away)

It's annoying to miss a game this early in the season, but I have no choice. There's no way of getting back from Reading to Birmingham by public transport after a game on a Wednesday night so I won't be making the trip to Berkshire.

Drogba's back from injury to make his first appearance of the season and it's him and Lampard who score the goals in a 2-1 win. It's a decent result. We're already four points clear of Manchester United, who've had two draws. A good start.

Sunday August 19
Liverpool (away)

I don't bother with this one either. I'm a bit fed up with Liverpool. Despite finishing above them in the league year after year and winning five league games out of six against them in the Mourinho-Benitez era, they just keep turning us over in important cup games – two Champions League semis and an FA Cup semi in the past three years. I also find the 'hilarious wit' of their fans a bit tiresome and it's a pain in the arse to get to Anfield from the city centre, particularly if you have to spend your time trying to not have a London accent.

I elect to watch this one in a pub. The Manchester derby is on beforehand, so I get there in time to watch both games. The pub seems to be home today to fans of Chelsea, Liverpool, Man United, Villa and Birmingham and the loudest cheer of the day comes when Alex Ferguson's scowling face is shown on the big screen after City score their winner at Eastlands. Even a near-by United fan has a wry smile on his face.

John Terry is back for us, having missed the start of the season injured, but Liverpool almost take the lead after two minutes. A quarter of an hour later they're in front through Torres. We look like we're going to struggle to pull back level until we get a generous decision in the second half. Malouda collides with Finnan and goes down and Rob Styles gives a penalty. It wasn't a foul but it wasn't a dive either – it was a collision that ended with Malouda being knocked over. Lampard slots the penalty away and we get a fortuitous draw.

Meanwhile United have no wins and only two points from three games. Looks like they could be on for a relegation battle.

Saturday August 25
Portsmouth (home)

Our fifth game of the season is the first one on a Saturday. Long gone are the days when all games, or even the vast majority, kicked off at 3pm on a Saturday.

Over the past year or so I've taken to walking to the Bridge from Victoria. For years I squeezed onto the crowded and sweaty District Line with everyone else, but when I began to travel down to London by coach on a regular basis an alarm bell went off in my head that said: "It only takes an hour to walk through one of the nicest parts of London. Why force yourself into a tiny gap under someone else's armpit on the Tube?"

So now, unless I'm short of time or it's raining, I walk. Through Belgravia and Sloane Square, wondering exactly where Jose's house is, along the King's Road and onto Fulham Road. Strolling along King's Road is always an experience – nice pubs, attractive women, exclusive shops I don't want to go into (and which might not let me even if I did) and a bit of minor celebrity spotting. In the past year I've seen Bill Wyman, Michael Schumacher, Gordon Ramsey, Eddie Jordan, and, er, Gloria Hunniford. I'll leave you to work out which of those I was most excited about, but as a clue, Gloria Hunniford didn't play bass on Get Off Of My Cloud.

Portsmouth are a decent side these days with the likes of David James and Sol Campbell in their team. Harry Redknapp has also taken Glen Johnson off our hands, which I won't be complaining about. He didn't blossom in the way he looked like he might and his defending in the goal-fest against Birmingham was one of the reasons it was a goal-fest. As a replacement we've signed Juliano Belletti, a Brazilian right-back from Barcelona, who scored their winner when they beat Arsenal in the Champions League final – surely enough to grant instant hero status.

David James always seems to play well against us, or at least he has since he dropped the ball at Di Matteo's feet in the 2000 FA Cup final against Villa. Today he makes a string of good saves but can do nothing about a Lampard piledriver after half an hour, set up by a clever back-heel from Drogba. It's the only goal.

The first month of the season finishes with us top of the league. Ten points from a possible 12 and we're eight clear of Man United, who are second bottom. Ok, they won the Charity Shield, but I'll let them have that if they stay 18 places below us. It's been a good August.

Chapter 2

All change

Sunday September 2
Aston Villa (away)

While home games mean travelling halfway across the country, Villa Park is a stadium I can walk to. But not today. I've arranged to meet Chris and John, who sit behind me, for a drink before the match. They discovered a pub they love in West Bromwich – near the Hawthorns – a couple of years back and return to it for every game in the Midlands.

So I meet them and John's girlfriend Shruti in this pub a couple of hours before kick-off. The main thing they love about the Hind is its curry. However, on Sundays it only does a barbecue. John and Chris are happy with this, but Shruti and I are vegetarians. I'm not overly bothered – I'm not that hungry – but Chris is indignant on our behalf. In his booming voice he takes them to task for not serving vegetarian food but to no avail. Funnily enough they have no plans to rewrite their food policy for him.

Then John says, "What about that curry we had? There's still some in the car." Shruti nips out of the pub and returns with a saucepan full of what's left of the beetroot curry they had for dinner last night, wherever they were. Who drives around with cold curry in the boot of their car?

John looks for cutlery but all he can find are some wooden chip forks. Apparently Shruti made the curry herself and it's lovely. But I'm somewhat wary – not many pubs let you eat your own food. And sure enough after a couple of minutes a passing barmaid spots us and lets rip. "You can't eat your own food in here!" she yells. "But you're refusing to provide food for vegetarians," replies Chris. I'm prepared to let it go, I don't want to cause trouble. Chris, John and Shruti put our case across but the barmaid is unrepentant. We can't eat it.

Sometimes you wonder how you came to find yourself in a certain situation. This is one of them.

I'm about to watch Chelsea play Aston Villa, and yet I'm in a pub near West Brom's ground, being shouted at for eating cold beetroot curry out of a saucepan with a wooden chip fork. The woman shouting at me is wearing a Woody Woodpecker t-shirt. How has my life come to this?

Once John and Chris have eaten up – and Shruti and I haven't – we leave for the ground in Chris's car. As we walk around Villa Park we pass Peter Withe. "Look it's Peter Withe," I say to John. He has no idea who Peter Withe is. "He scored the winner when Villa won the European Cup in 1982," I tell him. John says he wasn't even born then. John was born in 1984. I feel old.

The game starts and we dominate the first half. We have several chances and get corner after corner – it must be close to double figures just in this first half. Villa have none. But they defend very well and that's the main reason it's 0-0 at half-time. Two minutes after the break Villa get their first corner, and score from it. We've been all over them and couldn't score, they have one chance and it's 1-0.

This brings out Villa's class and they play much better in this half. Jose throws on Pizarro, Joe Cole and Kalou – a clear sign of attacking intent – but we fail to make any real chances, while Villa get stronger and still defend superbly. Two minutes from the end Villa break, Ashley Young shoots across goal and Agbonlahor knocks it in. 2-0. Unbelievable.

We've had 20 shots to their nine and 13 corners to their two. But Villa put the ball in the net and defended very well and we failed on both counts.

Ludicrously the rail line for the short trip back to Birmingham New Street is closed, leaving me to walk home in the rain. What conversations do they have? "Hmmm... Villa are at home. Let's do engineering works..."

Living up here means that unlike most Chelsea fans I work with several Villa supporters. As I trudge along getting soaked I start to hear from them. My colleague Zoe texts me to ask if Villa really have won 2-0 – she's out and has been told it's 2-0 but can't believe it. I reply to say it's true and that while we dominated much of the game we couldn't score and Villa did, so fair enough. She replies saying she loves me for being an honest football fan. This makes me chuckle, despite my mood and the weather both being foul. Because a few months ago she called me "a football Hitler" – whatever one of those is.

Saturday September 15
Blackburn (home)

It's a 5.15pm kick-off today because the game is on television. As I walk towards the ground in the bright afternoon sunshine, listening to the conclusion of the 3pm starts on my radio, this late kick-off lark seems a thoroughly good idea. If, that is, you overlook the fact the game is on Setanta, who have secured the rights to show one Premier League game each weekend, meaning anyone who wants to see every match now has to take out two subscriptions. What a cracking move that was.

Dan can't come today, so in his seat is Mark's girlfriend Anna, from Australia and attending her first match. She's impressed at how big the crowd is and how everyone comes to the game in the team colours. Let's hope Chelsea make it memorable for her. If we win today we'll go level on points at the top with Arsenal, despite that loss to Villa.

We bombard the Blackburn goal but Brad Friedel, as so often, is in inspired form and makes a string of great saves. In the second half Kalou manages to get the ball in the net and we all think we've finally broken the deadlock but it's ruled offside. Jose goes berserk on the touchline, which might suggest it's a bad decision, or might just suggest Jose is getting excitable as usual.

There's time for Friedel to make one last amazing save from a Shevchenko header and we finish 0-0. Anna says she's enjoyed the game but Mark is disappointed the team haven't treated her to a goal.

We've played well, even if we haven't won, and this is with Lampard and Drogba both still missing through injury. We've steadied the ship after the Villa defeat and hopefully our two main goal threats will be back soon. It's two dropped points, but it could be a lot worse.

Tuesday September 18
Rosenborg (home)

The day starts in lively fashion with Jose's pre-match press conference, where he comes out with this gem: "The style of how we play is very important. But it is omelettes and eggs. No eggs – no omelettes! It depends on the quality of the eggs. In the supermarket you have class one, two or class three eggs and some are more expensive than others and some give you better omelettes. So when the class one eggs are in Waitrose and you cannot go there, you have a problem."

Classic Mourinho. Typical of him to be creative and eloquent enough to compare his players to eggs, but also typical of him to be having a dig at Roman for not letting him buy more players. We have bought a few over the past three or four years...

I make my way down to the match after work. As soon as I'm on the District Line it's clear there aren't many people about tonight. It's £36 a ticket, cheaper than normal but still steep for a game against Norwegians. And it seems a lot of people have decided not to come. There are only about 24,000 here, our lowest crowd for years.

Hardly any of the normal gang are present. I have six empty seats to my right and seven to my left. You can tell that some of those who are here have never been before. The bloke behind me keeps getting the words to songs wrong and at one point his girlfriend asks what the fans in the West Stand are chanting and he says, "It's something about Marks and Spencers." It was "Loyal supporters".

Drogba, Lampard and Carvalho are all still missing, but we've still got too much quality for Rosenborg and are dominant. And just like against Villa and Blackburn dominance doesn't mean goals. Amazingly, Rosenborg's first attack does. With 24 minutes gone, they get a free kick, a cross comes over and defender Miika Koppinen volleys it home. We continue to bombard them but it's still 1-0 at half time. With none of the usual crowd around to talk to – with the exception of a suited and booted straight-from-work Big Sam, who I'm unable to talk to because he doesn't know me – I find myself crowd-watching in the break. There's a bloke two rows back doing a Sudoku puzzle. This is a strange, strange night.

We start the second half still constantly attacking and Sheva gets us level after 53 minutes. Surely now the floodgates will open? Well, no. Malouda and Kalou both hit the woodwork but we can't score. By the end John Terry is playing up front. It finishes 1-1. Although we've attacked all game we haven't played well. There's a lack of creativity and things are not going to plan. The frustration at this, plus the fact we've all paid £36 to watch this rubbish, probably explains the boos on the final whistle. I join in. For the first time in the Mourinho era I boo the team. I feel bad about it but this has been dismal. I've done a full day's work before coming down here and I'll get home at about 2am. And at least I'm here, unlike many others. I've earned the right to have my say.

Wednesday September 19

Not surprisingly, the papers are full of egg references. The Independent and Express have both got Mourinho "left with egg on his face", the Mail declares Sheva a "good egg" for rescuing the point and most imaginatively the Times gives its ratings for the players in eggs. The only one to get three eggs – "grade A, tastier than a Michel Roux soufflé" – is Shevchenko.

Surprisingly the Sun is an ovum-free zone – it's gone for Sheva Me Timbers.

I chat to dad on the phone during the evening and tell him I can't see Jose still being in charge at the end of the season, maybe even not by Christmas. "Do you really think he'd quit?" dad asks. "No, I can't see him walking out," I say, "If he quits he won't get a pay-off. But I think Abramovich will sack him."

I watch the Rangers v Stuttgart Champions League game on Sky, because I don't want to watch Arsenal or Man United, then find myself flicking through the channels for a while. I'm about to go to bed just after midnight when I wander on to Sky Sports News and spot the yellow breaking news ticker along the bottom of the screen.

It says, "**REPORTS – JOSE MOURINHO HAS LEFT CHELSEA.**"

Bugger.

After a few seconds of watching, it becomes clear they haven't got it confirmed but it's true. Soon an unnamed senior player has told them Mourinho has told him he's been sacked. I stick Five Live on too and it's the topic of discussion on their late-night show. The BBC is being less cautious than Sky and presenting the news as fact, not just unsubstantiated reports. It really has happened – Jose has gone. I've never been so unhappy at being proved right so quickly.

Pat Nevin says on the radio how disappointed he is and how he can't see the move benefiting the club. When listeners call in it's not only distraught Chelsea fans; a surprisingly fair and reasonable Liverpool supporter says he'll miss Mourinho as a character in the English game and is glad he's gone because Liverpool feared him. A Manchester United fan agrees. What better proof could you have that this is bad news for Chelsea than the fact our biggest rivals are delighted?

Dan texts me discussing the news and after about an hour of watching Sky and listening to the radio with my mouth open slack-jawed, trying to take the news in, I decide to go to bed.

Nothing's going to change. Dan's message proves to be the first of many during the night. I'm woken up a couple of times by friends texting to say how shocked they are, including my apparently nocturnal ex-flatmate Damian at 4.30am. Thanks, people.

Personally I'm not shocked. It's been coming for months and even if there hadn't already been the rumblings of discontent, look at the club's track record. Ruud Gullit sacked in the midst of a title challenge, months after winning our first trophy in 26 years. Gianluca Vialli went three months after winning his third trophy in two-and-a-half years in charge and Claudio Ranieri was out on his ear days after leading us to second place in the league and the Champions League semi-finals. Any club that can do all that can sack anyone.

But that doesn't make this anything other than terrible news. The man has led us to two league titles in three seasons when all his predecessors put together managed one in 99 years. He's won six major trophies while the rest combined only won eight. Yet we see fit to get rid of him. What a terrible mistake.

What does Abramovich think will happen now? I suppose he'll go out and get one of the managers who are available and better than Mourinho. Oh hang on, no he won't, because there aren't any. Pat Nevin summed it up brilliantly on Five Live: "I think probably Abramovich looks at Barcelona and watches the way they play and thinks 'Hey, I'd like my team to play that way', but just about any team in the planet's history would like their team to play the way Barcelona play just now. It's not that easy to get players of that quality and that style into your side."

Sometimes Roman, you don't know what you've got till it's gone.

Thursday September 20

I'm getting ready for work when they announce on Five Live that Jose will be replaced by Avram Grant, the anonymous director of football who arrived in the summer, having filled the same role at Portsmouth. I assume this is as a caretaker, but it soon becomes apparent that it's not. Chelsea's new permanent manager is Avram Grant, whose managerial experience is in the Israeli league. It gets worse.

At work it's all anyone wants to talk to me about. Everyone asks what's going on and I don't know. The texts and emails continue all day. Fans of all teams seem stunned.

The one good thing is Steve Clarke seems to be staying. I'm very thankful for that – he's Mr Chelsea – but I wouldn't blame him if he left, either now or to join Jose when he gets a job somewhere else.

Hundreds of fans head to Stamford Bridge to protest during the day. If I didn't have to be at work 100 miles away, I'd be there too.

Friday September 21

Jose breaks his silence today, presumably having been unable to speak until his compensation deal was brokered. He maintains he left "by mutual consent" but I wonder how much financial pressure has been put on him to say that. The story – from him but especially from Chelsea – seems to be that the working relationship between him and everyone else had broken down and they all, Jose included, decided it was time to bring it to an end.

If that's true I wish they'd tried a bit harder to sort it out. It was worth fighting for, the success we've had in the past three years shows that.

In his press conference Jose looks relaxed, like a weight is off his mind. He says he's happy to have left. I hope that's just pride speaking and not the truth. He also says he's happy with what he achieved at Chelsea. We all were, Jose.

He'll be back to haunt us. He'll get a top job somewhere and when he does he'll come back to sign some of his old favourites. Most of the team look like they would crawl over broken glass for Jose. That spirit and loyalty has been one of our strengths under him, one of the things that's taken us to trophy after trophy. Wherever Jose goes next, he'll want to sign Lampard, Drogba, Carvalho, Essien, Terry. Some of them will go, I'm sure. I hope it's not in the January transfer window; that would completely take the wheels off our season, which is already looking in disarray.

I still can't believe this has happened. The man is a charismatic, brilliant, successful genius and we don't want him in charge? What madness is that? All we have left is the hope that the team spirit he created can live on. And our memories of a hatful of trophies, especially two league titles. The first championships in my lifetime and, after this week's madness, probably the only ones. Thanks for everything Jose. I feel really bad about having booed on Tuesday.

Saturday September 22

The papers are full of stories of a mass exodus of players. It wouldn't surprise me at all. Not only do they suggest half the team will be off at the first opportunity, they also talk of massive splits in the changing room, with most players distraught at Jose's departure and a small handful happy, perhaps culpable. What a mess.

I put a fiver on Guus Hiddink being our manager on the first day of next season, at 4/1.

Sunday September 23
Manchester United (away)

Marcel Marceau has died. Hope they don't hold a minute's mime before the match.

One of the good things about having moved to Birmingham is it greatly reduces the distance for travelling to games oop north. By the time I've caught the coach at 11.15am a lot of Chelsea fans will have already been travelling up from London and the Home Counties for a couple of hours. Come to think of it so will a lot of Man United fans.

On my way to the coach station I pass a crowd of about 50 people gathered outside Primark before it's even opened. A small part of me wishes I was joining them instead of heading off to a stadium full of idiots for a game we'll almost certainly lose. As a token protest against what the club has done over the past few days I've decided not to wear my Chelsea shirt, or anything that makes me obviously a Chelsea fan. I've got a blue shirt on, but then lots of people wear blue shirts, and – hopefully – nobody can see my Chelsea boxer shorts.

My decision feels like the right one when a typically cocky-looking United fan gets on the coach a minute or so after me. I'm in no mood for any banter.

When I reach Manchester I find for the second away game running the train companies have decided to close the railway station next to the ground, so I catch the tram. By the time we reach Exchange Quays it's absolutely pouring with rain, clichéd both for Manchester and my mood.

I can't stand Old Trafford. The sheer size of the stadium is very impressive, I'll admit that, but that's about the only positive thing I can say. The whole place seems stuck in a time warp - and not in a good way. They always seem to play Status Quo, though on this occasion they've moved forward a few years. As I walk to my seat I can hear a several-months-old Justin Timberlake song followed by a Beyonce number from the same 'era'. At most grounds they play rousing songs to get the crowd singing, here someone sticks Now 65 in the CD player and hits 'play'.

They also don't have a big screen, which is not the end of the world, but it's become so common these days that several teams in the Championship have them and the self-proclaimed biggest club in the world doesn't. And the guy who makes the announcements has real trouble pronouncing certain names – a bit of an issue if your job is to read out footballers' names. He's always found Cudicini impossible and used to pronounce Geremi as "Jeram-eye" instead of "Jeram-ee".

I'm in the very back row, so directly behind me I have a hospitality box – cue the prawn sandwich cliché. I'm not impressed with this, but console myself with the thought I might impede their view every time I stand up.

Shortly before kick-off some nobody comes out on to the pitch to sing his hopelessly contrived version of Take Me Home Country Roads, cleverly reworked into Take Me Home United Road. The atmosphere here makes me cringe.

Cech has to make a stunning save from Rooney after two minutes but overall we start quite well, easily matching United without creating anything more than a couple of half-chances. But they don't either, and it's a promising start, until after half-an-hour Mikel goes in for a 50-50 tackle with Evra and referee Mike Dean pulls out a red card. It looks an inexplicable decision and for the first time I'm pleased to have the prawn sandwich boys behind me as, along with several other fans, I turn to watch the action replay on the TV in the corner of their box. It confirms how harsh it was; a definite foul but not a bad one. To give them their due, the United fans in the box shrug their shoulders and hold their hands up in the air to say "No, I don't know what that was about either..."

After that we're completely up against it. Ten against 11 is tough anywhere, but away to the champions when you're in a bit of a mess anyway, it's really tricky. But we look like we're about to hold out until half-time. The fourth official says there's two minutes of stoppage time and then, after three minutes, United score. It's the first goal in red for everyone's favourite controversially transferred legend Carlos Tevez. Where did that third minute come from? From the Old Trafford Seam of Added Time When They're Not Winning of course, a mine not even Thatcher could have closed.

Off the field I've been disappointed. Our fans, myself included, have hardly stopped singing, in huge contrast to the United muppets. But I'd expected there to be a load of chanting of Mourinho's name, and instead it's happened once. I know we have to move on, just not this quickly. The club is bigger than one man, but what the club has done over the past few days ought to have sparked more protest. While we have to move on soon, today there ought to be some form of support for the greatest manager we've ever had. Ten seconds of singing his name isn't enough.

One tiny group even started to chant "Avram Grant's blue and white army", but thankfully they were given short shrift by the rest of us. The most common chant of the day is "Stevie Clarke's blue and white army". I'll take that, it's meant to suggest we're not even acknowledging Grant's presence.

In the second half we look content to restrict the damage to 1-0. Joey Cole and Malouda are brought back deeper and Sheva is on his own up front. This doesn't make life easy for him but it has to be said that in his first game with a mate in charge rather than a genius who doubted him, he's turning in one of his worst performances for Chelsea. Kalou and Pizarro come on for Sheva and Cole and we offer a little more threat but there's a noticeable difference from the Mourinho days. When we were chasing a game under Jose, he used to take off defenders and chuck forwards on. Today we sit back with nine men behind the ball and settle for 1-0. I know we're down to ten men against Manchester United, but is this really the attractive attacking football we were supposedly being deprived under Mourinho?

In the 90th minute Ben-Haim goes vaguely near Luis Saha, who goes flying like an Olympic highboard champ. I expect a yellow card for diving but they get a penalty. Unbelievable, and entirely in keeping with the way this match has gone. Again we all turn to watch the TV in the prawn sandwich box and it confirms what we saw from the back of the stand but the ref didn't – it was a shocking dive. Saha puts the penalty away. 2-0, game over. People are leaving in droves and the man next to me ceremonially rips off the cover of his programme and tears it into shreds, in the style of an angry cartoon character. In a broad Northern Irish accent he screams at the blokes in the box "You should be ashamed!" They laugh and, absolutely fuming, I join him, shouting "You should be ashamed of your club" at them. Of course, it's probably not their club at all. They're there as a reward for selling more central heating units than anyone else in their region last month, or in the hope they might put some business the way of their hosts.

Then I remember I'm actually fairly ashamed of my club this week and realise the futility of it all. And so I do something I've only ever done once before in my life – leave a Chelsea game early. There's only a few seconds left but I've seen more than enough. It means not staying to applaud the players but so be it. I can't stand to be there a second longer.

It's still bucketing down with rain and I get soaked all over again heading for the tram. My coach gets stuck in traffic on the outskirts of the city, giving me plenty of time to dry out because by the time I get back to Birmingham it's almost an hour late. I arrive home at 11pm, meaning I've missed the highlights on Match of the Day 2. It's probably for the best, my blood pressure is high enough as it is. I just feel let down by football all round. By Chelsea's management, by the inept refereeing, by the diving of Saha and by the short memories of some of the Chelsea fans. None of them deserve me.

What a contrast. Last week it was a stroll to the game in sunny weather ahead of conversations about what a big crowd there was and how everyone was wearing the shirt. This week it's pissing down, the journey takes forever, the half-empty stadium from Tuesday is still fresh in the memory and I felt too ashamed to wear the shirt. Right now, if you told me I could never go to a football match ever again, I wouldn't really be all that bothered.

Wednesday September 26
Hull City (away)

Grant's second match in charge is a Carling Cup game away to Championship side Hull. A potential banana skin, if ever there was one. One of the many impressive things about the Mourinho era was the way we used to never slip on these banana skins.

The game is live on Sky and I watch it at home. For the first time in ages Chelsea turn in a thoroughly professional performance, although again it takes a while to score. When we go in front after 37 minutes it's a first goal for the club for teenager Scott Sinclair. In the second half two goals from Kalou and one from Sidwell, also his first for the club, make it 4-0. A satisfactory win, an upset avoided. But it will take more than swatting aside lower division opposition to make me think we're on the right track.

Saturday September 29
Fulham (home)

Avram Grant's first home game in charge sees a big banner bearing Jose Mourinho's name unfurled in the Shed End. Quite right too. But I bet they won't be allowed to bring that back again.

It's the first chance to discuss the changes in person with my neighbours and we are all agreed that what has happened in the past 10 days is just amazing. There are various opinions; most think it's an awful mistake, some say we need to move on and get behind the new man, and some even criticise Jose for going a few days before the United game. I'm wearing a hastily-mail-ordered "**BRING BACK MOURINHO**" T-shirt. I think that just about sums up my feelings. I know he won't be brought back, but it's a catchier slogan than "**OH MY GOD, WHAT ON EARTH HAVE YOU DONE? YOU'VE SACKED THE BEST MANAGER WE'VE EVER HAD!**"

Drogba is back and plays alongside Shevchenko up front. Sheva nearly puts us in front after two minutes but doesn't and after a few minutes the chants of Jose's name start. I join in. Both sets of players look like they couldn't score in a brothel.

Things get even worse when Terry fails to reappear for the second half. He took a bang to the head before the break and it turns out he's fractured a cheekbone. How long will he be out for? We're already without Carvalho, Lampard and Essien. We're on top in the second half but look like we won't score if we play until midnight. And things go from bad to worse to even-worse-than-that when Drogba gets sent off. Fulham have three good chances to get a winner and by the end we're holding on and lucky to get a 0-0 draw. We've now gone 67 league games unbeaten at home, but we were lucky to get a point at the Bridge to Fulham.

The players are booed off, although I doubt most people are booing the team. The targets are higher up the chain of command. I have to take a second to remind myself that we recently won the league two years running and last season came second and won both cups. Looking at what we've become – a club in disarray with a struggling team and irate, bitterly let-down, frustrated fans – you'd be forgiven for forgetting. On the way out of the ground we discuss recent form. At the moment we're losing away and drawing at home. Keep that up for a whole season and you'll finish on 19 points...

Chapter 3

Picking up the pieces

Monday October 1

My afternoon is brightened up by an email from ChelseamegastoreUSA.com offering me a choice of three T-shirts commemorating Chelsea's summer tour of America, all reduced (ie they can't sell them to the American fans) at $11.99 each. Yes, dollars not pounds. Why have I been sent this email? And does nothing related to this club have anything to do with football fans from England anymore?

Wednesday October 3
Valencia (away)

For the second time in six months we're away to Valencia in the Champions League. It's an attractive fixture at a good stadium in a lovely city and I'd like to be there. But, just as when we beat them in the quarter-finals in April, the gap between the draw being made and the match itself was too short for me to organise the time off.

Tonight will tell a lot about what state we are really in under Avram Grant. He lost his first big test, but to be fair the game at Old Trafford was just days after he took over. The performance against Fulham wasn't good and you have to think if we play like that in Valencia we'll get squashed as easily as one of that city's famous oranges. John Terry is playing, wearing one of those Phantom of the Opera masks. It would take a severed head to keep him off the pitch, not just a fractured cheekbone.

Valencia almost take the lead in the first minute but we're not reprieved for long. After nine minutes the ball bounces off Essien to the excellent David Villa and he slots it past Cech. This is not looking good. After 20 minutes Cech makes a great save from Joaquin and we're on the rack.

Then, out of nowhere, we're level. A great exchange of passes between Malouda and Drogba sees the winger knock over a perfect cross for Joe Cole to touch in. We haven't deserved it, but the abilities to withstand pressure and to get a goal when not playing well were two of the hallmarks of the Mourinho era and we've shown them both tonight.

Valencia have chances to go back in front and don't take them. As the second half progresses, we start to play better and better. With 20 minutes left we get our reward when Joe Cole wins the ball near the halfway line and plays a great through ball with the outside of his right foot for Drogba to run on to. Looking back to the form of last season, Drogba finishes clinically.

Valencia throw the kitchen sink at us but we hold on for a fantastic win. It's the second time this year we've won 2-1 in this stadium, but in very different circumstances. Back then we were on a roll, had momentum and a top manager determined to win the Champions League. This time round we're in a state of shock and led by a virtually unknown Israel who looks like Baron Greenback off Dangermouse. But the baron has achieved the first big win of his Chelsea career tonight. It's a great win – hats off to him and the players.

Sunday October 7
Bolton (away)

I'm at work, making this the first match I won't be able to see either in person or on TV since Reading away in mid-August. I have to work occasional weekends – about one a month – and my mate Simon, who does our rotas, usually manages to do me proud, giving me weekends when we're somewhere like Bolton rather than leaving me stuck in the office when we're at home.

I manage to keep across what's going on thanks to the internet and am pleased to see Lampard back in the team for the first time since Portsmouth six weeks ago. It's no coincidence that was the last time we won a league game. We've lost two and drawn two without him, not even scoring since Frank got the goal against Pompey. It really shows how much we've missed him. We're starting the day in 10th place, unheard of for us in recent years.

Shortly before half-time Kalou puts us one up with our first league goal for 460 minutes. It's enough to clinch the game and it's a good win. The first league victory of the Avram Grant era and only our fourth in the nine games we've played in the league this season. It lifts us to seventh, only a point off fourth place, but seven points behind leaders Arsenal, having played a game more. We've already got a mountain to climb if we're going to get anywhere near the top of the league.

Saturday October 20
Middlesbrough (away)

Who can think of anywhere better to spend their birthday than the Riverside Stadium? I can for starters. And that's why when we kick off in the North East I'm about 300 miles away on the beach in East Sussex.

With my 32nd birthday falling on a Saturday I'd planned to spend the evening having a few drinks in Birmingham with friends from work, then rugby intervened. Much to everyone's surprise the apparently rubbish England team contrived to get through to the Rugby World Cup final. I'm not a rugby fan at all, in fact I can't stand it, and sharing drinking space on my birthday with a load of Tarquins singing Swing Low Sweet Chariot and behaving like the toffs they are or want to be is not my idea of a good time. With some of my friends keen to watch the game – and I wouldn't be uncharitable enough to try to stop them – even the option of a rugby-free pub is not on the cards.

So at a couple of day's notice I head down to see my parents and my sister and her family instead. That's why, as Alex puts us

1-0 up, I'm trying to show my two-year-old nephew Toby how to throw stones into the sea. I don't detach myself completely – I check the scores on my phone every few minutes – and by the time we get home I know Drogba's made it 2-0.

I assume the goal from centre-back Alex is a header from a set-piece so I'm delighted to watch Match of the Day later and discover it's a screamer of a free-kick from a mile out. John Terry may have many qualities, but he can't do that.

This may have been an odd and troubled season for Chelsea, but at least they've remembered to give me a happy birthday.

Wednesday October 24
Schalke (home)

I've only missed two Chelsea home games in Europe since I was born. I've been helped with that statistic by the fact we didn't qualify for Europe until I was 18, but nonetheless it's a fact I'm proud of. The first I missed was the very first one, Viktoria Zizkov in the Cup Winners' Cup first round in 1994, which was due to teenage me not getting my act together. But the second was one of the unmissable ones – Milan in the Champions League under Vialli in 1999. My excuse that time? On holiday in Tenerife, booked before the draw was made. I watched it in a very nice bar, quaffing San Miguel, but it wasn't the same.

Tonight I miss number three and it's through choice. When Mourinho left I decided I wanted to make some small stand against the club. And without a great deal of ammunition at my disposal, I decided to miss the next home game I had to buy a ticket for. So I watch on TV. Despite the great win in Valencia it's still vital we win, partly because of the dropped points against Rosenborg. And we get off to the best of starts – after four minutes an average shot from Florent Malouda goes straight between the German keeper's legs and we're 1-0 up.

A couple of minutes into the second half a great diving header from Drogba makes it 2-0. He's been the most vocal opponent among the players of the recent changes and some of the fans booed him tonight, but let's face it, who connected to Chelsea isn't frustrated by what's happened? Plenty of people are being big enough to say "The club comes first, let's move on" and fair enough if they are, but don't pretend it hasn't affected you at all. Drogba has been honest.

At 2-0 up we look comfortable but there's still one last scare when Schalke's Larsen hammers a header against the post and the ball rebounds straight into the relieved Cech's hands. Maybe luck is on our side tonight?

Two wins and a draw from our first three European games. If you'd offered me that at the start I'd have taken it – and I would have assumed the draw would have been out in Valencia. I hesitate to ask it, but has Grant patched up Mourinho's mess?

Saturday October 27
Manchester City (home)

City have had a great start under Sven Goran Eriksson and are one of the teams above us in the league that we'll have to get past if this isn't to be an awful season. But it won't be easy. They beat Man United and even if we win today we'll still be a point behind them.

It appears Chelsea are taking steps to get the fans back on side, or at least remind us it's the team we support, not the ex-manager. There are free flags for everyone again – that usually happens on big European nights – and new video montages of great moments from our past play on the big screens before kick-off. There's one set to London Calling by the Clash, showing some of our legendary ex-players and triumphs from way back, the cup victories of the seventies, the league winners from 1955 and the likes of Nevin, Dixon, Walker, Vialli, Zola and Hughes scoring cracking goals. The other is set to I Guess That's Why They Call It The Blues by Elton John and concentrates more on the triumphs of this decade. I'm sure the timing is not accidental – the singing of Jose Mourinho's name and the chants of "Stevie Clarke's blue and white army" during the last home league game against Fulham illustrated how unhappy the fans were. The club has obviously decided to take the opportunity to remind people that this is still Chelsea, with or without Mourinho, that it's still the club of Osgood, Dixon and Zola, and that those of us who were here pre-Jose and long before should remember it.

We start well and are in front after a quarter of an hour when Lampard plays in Essien with a good pass and he slots the ball past Joe Hart. And on the half hour Lamps plays an even better pass – an absolutely sublime ball that curls round Richard Dunne and evades Micah Richards' toes by inches, straight into the path of Drogba who gleefully knocks it home. It would win pass of the season if there was such a thing. City have a couple of decent chances in this half, but we also have two fairly good penalty shouts turned down. We could easily have been 4-0 up at half time – we're playing really well.

Ten minutes after the break it's 3-0 through Drogba. About a minute later Didier misses a golden chance for a hat-trick and we are absolutely rampant. On the hour it's 4-0 thanks to Joe Cole. Kalou makes it 5-0 after 75 and in injury time Sheva, on as sub, adds a sixth. We have been absolutely brilliant and have played a good Man City side off the pitch.

In those three brilliant years under Jose we didn't once score six in a league game. We beat Macclesfield 6-1 in the cup last season but we only even scored five in the league once, a 5-1 win against Bolton. We got four countless times but then always seemed to shut up shop. Today we were superb, virtually unstoppable and playing wonderful football. What's happened?

After standing round for a few minutes discussing the miracle we've just seen, we go our separate ways. As I walk along King's Road in the sunshine I unfurl my flag and let it wave in the light breeze. Drivers honk their horns as they pass. A woman selling the Big Issue asks me the score. When I tell her, she cheers. And then as I pass a cafe, an excitable middle-aged Italian man sitting outside asks me the score. "We won 6-0!" I tell him. "Six?

Six? Chelsea won 6-0?" he replies, in disbelief. He gets out of his seat and hugs me.

The sun is shining, we've won 6-0, we've played brilliantly and the whole world is happy. It's tempting to say "Jose who?" Just this once...

Wednesday October 31
Leicester (home)

I've got a soft spot for Leicester City. I went to university in Leicester, spent three very happy years there and made several visits to Filbert Street. I wasn't being unfaithful to Chelsea, I was sports editor of the university newspaper, The Ripple, and used to get into the press box to do match reports. What 21-year-old would-be journalist would turn down the chance to watch Premiership football every other weekend for free, perched alongside the proper hacks?

I used to go to a lot of Chelsea matches too. In my final year I went to well over 30 games, a combination of Chelsea, Leicester and Brighton – I had a mate who was a Seagulls fan and I went with him to away matches in the Midlands. No wonder I left university with a load of debts and a 2:2.

Don't get me wrong though, I have no divided loyalties. I like Leicester more than most other clubs, but if they played Chelsea 1,000 times I would want Chelsea to win every one.

The Leicester I used to watch were a good side led by Martin O'Neill. But now they're searching for their third manager of the season and languish in the bottom half of the Championship, so we should see them off with no trouble.

Six minutes gone, Chelsea 0 Leicester 1.

Thankfully, we have Lampard and two goals from Super Frank put us in front. It stays that way for a while and looks fairly straightforward, we certainly come closest to adding to the score. But then after 69 minutes the recalled Shaun Wright-Phillips performs an unnecessary overhead kick somewhere near the right-back position, the ball goes to a Leicester player and a few seconds and a few crisp passes later it's 2-2. Five minutes later we're 3-2 down, through ex-Wimbledon and Newcastle carthorse Carl Cort.

Avram may have brought us our first 6-0 win for a decade, but he looks like he's about to furnish us with something else we haven't had for donkeys years – a home defeat to a lower division team. We're three minutes from going out when Andriy Shevchenko powers home the kind of goal we bought him to score and it looks like he's earned us extra time. Phew. Then in the third minute of stoppage time the sort of goalmouth scramble I haven't seen since I was scuffing around in the playground ends with the ball in the Leicester net. It's anyone's guess who scored – first it looks like Sheva, then it seems his shot hit Belletti on the way in and eventually it turns out a header by Frank that was cleared earlier in the melee was actually over the line. The goal is his, giving him a hat-trick.

We're in the last eight, we've narrowly avoided an upset and above all else we've followed a 6-0 masterclass with an incident-filled seven-goal thriller. Things really have changed, haven't they?

Chapter 4

Sleepless in Trondheim

Thursday November 1

While mooching around on Facebook, the social networking website, I notice the "Bring Back Jose Mourinho" group has "13 fewer members".

Saturday November 3
Wigan (away)

I fancied going to this game. I've never been to Wigan, it's cheap, we've got loads of tickets because they can't give them away to home fans, it's at 3pm on a Saturday and – according to a fanzine I picked up at the Man City game – the fans are targeting this as a day of celebrating how it used to be in the old days, for many of the reasons I've just listed.

But sadly it was sandwiched between two night shifts and the thought of leaving work at 6am, travelling to Wigan hoping to sleep on the train, trying to stay awake through what should be a straightforward win, travelling home again and being back at work for 10pm without having been to bed, well that's a bit much. Sorry if that makes me sound like a part-timer.

I make do with listening to it on Five Live. And it does indeed sound like a straightforward win – Lampard puts us ahead with yet another goal, his 97th for us, then Belletti makes it 2-0 with what sounds like a cracking goal. We have our seventh straight win.

With Arsenal and Manchester United having fought out a 2-2 win earlier, we're only three points behind the pair of them in third. Not bad for a team in disarray. Was I really saying we were unquestionably out of the title race as recently as a few minutes before we took the lead last Saturday? Watching the game on Match of the Day at work, I see Belletti's goal really was a belter. He's looking good in every game – what a shame he isn't five years younger.

Tuesday November 6
Schalke (away)

Wins in our past two matches have put us in a good position in the Champions League but it's never going to be easy away to the German champions. Schalke begin well and Belletti has to clear a shot off the line after Cech drops a corner. But arguably more worrying than our poor start is the fact that Cech has to have lengthy treatment on a leg injury.

Shortly before the break Joe Cole sets up Drogba for a half-decent chance but the keeper blocks it and that's about the only time we threaten in this half. We've had no answer for the Vorsprung Durch Technik of the Germans other than a bit of slightly fortunate panicky defending. Belletti may have cleared that ball off the line but apart from that he's been all over the place. My praise on Saturday must have cursed him.

Cech doesn't come out after the break but the fact we have as good a reserve keeper as Carlo Cudicini is always a comfort. But great as Carlo is, he needs the woodwork to save him a couple of times in the second half. We hold on for 0-0, probably undeserved. But it's a good result and, coupled with Rosenborg winning 2-0 in Valencia (maybe our draw against them wasn't such a bad result?), we only need a point from our last two games to qualify.

Meanwhile Liverpool, who were nearly out after taking one point from their first three games, beat Besiktas 8-0. It overshadows our goalless draw a bit.

Sunday November 11
Everton (home)

I've had a varied – and good – weekend in London. Yesterday I returned to the place of my birth, Leyton, to see Orient draw 1-1 with Bristol Rovers in the FA Cup and followed that by meeting some friends for my first-ever trip to a casino. Having managed not to lose my shirt (or any other garments) I kip on the sofa in my mate Ralfe's north London flat before heading to the Bridge. It makes a lovely change to only have to get the Piccadilly and District lines to a match.

Today's essential-player-injury-victim is Ricardo Carvalho, who goes up for a header with Yakubu, lands awkwardly and needs treatment on his back. He comes back on but can only hobble about in midfield so there seems little point him staying on. Thankfully after about five minutes Grant sees sense and Ricky is off. How long can our injury list get?

We have a few chances before finally going in front with 20 minutes left when Drogba heads home a Kalou corner. It's so rare for us to score from corners, maybe Kalou should take them more often? That looks like it's given us a hard-earned three points until, in the final minute, a McFadden shot is deflected and loops up into the air where Tim Cahill executes a fantastic overhead kick from six yards which Carlo has absolutely no chance of saving.

Yet another draw at home. Everton are good but this is still a disappointing result, particularly as we led with seconds to go. We're not far behind Man United and Arsenal, but with results like this there's no chance of closing the gap.

The mood is lightened slightly when, as we leave the ground, Mark spots Big Sam in our path. He engineers a textbook manoeuvre. Approaching the great man sideways on, Mark pretends to have to shuffle around him to avoid walking into him and does so by placing a hand on each of Sam's shoulders. We make our way out into the rain giggling like small children. "I touched Big Sam!" says a delighted Mark. I can't help but be impressed by the way he pulled that off. It was the most skilful thing anyone in a blue shirt managed all day.

Friday November 23

England lost 3-2 at home to Croatia on Wednesday, when we only needed a draw to qualify for Euro 2008. Not surprisingly Steve McClaren lost his job yesterday and today's papers are full of speculation about who will take over. Jose is one of the main names being put forward.

I don't think he'd take the job, but I hope he gets it. Firstly, he'd be very good and secondly, if he moves into international football he won't be able to come back and sign our best players. Please, England, go for Jose.

Saturday November 24
Derby (away)

I've been to Derby twice before and both times it ended in disappointment. I saw us lose 3-2 at the Baseball Ground when Frank Leboeuf was sent off, Ruud Gullit broke his ankle and Ashley Ward scored a last-minute winner. My other trip to this fine city was for an audition for the quiz show 15 to 1, when I was a student with time on my hands and a decent grasp of general knowledge. Or so I thought. I got asked four questions and the only one I knew was "What number is at the bottom of a dartboard?" It's three. I left them thinking I knew nothing about anything other than darts and never got put to the test by William G. Stewart.

It's good to have another away game in the Midlands. It takes less than an hour to get here by train and I've arranged to meet up with Dan for a drink. His train from London is due in before mine so when I arrive I call him to find out where he is. "Turn right and go down the road and I'm in the first pub, the Brewster's Arms," he tells me.

I come out of the station and turn right. There are three pubs opposite the station. None are called the Brewster's Arms. I call him back but get no answer. One pub, the Merry Widows, is full of Chelsea fans so I head over, maybe Dan got mixed up with names and he's in here. I can't see him but buy a pint anyway. Then Dan phones me to find out where I am. I try to explain and he points out that he said "Go down the road and I'm in the first pub..." I didn't go down the road. He avoided the pubs by the station, knowing they would be busy.

Dan wanders down to meet me outside the Merry Widows and we walk to the ground. On the way he points out the pub he'd been in. It's called the Brunswick Inn. Not the Brewster's Arms. How would I have found it anyway?

Carvalho's injury still rules him out but Terry is back for the first time since he got injured on England duty five weeks ago. He and the rest of our England players get a load of abuse from the Derby fans for "letting the country down", as is often the way with supporters of clubs whose last England international wore baggy shorts and got paid the maximum wage. Their own team are very poor and bottom of the table. We don't play well but cruise to a comfortable 2-0 win with goals from Kalou and Wright-Phillips.

As I make my way back to the station I realise I've been walking in completely the wrong direction for five minutes and have to turn round, go back past the stadium and then take the correct route. Away trips in the Midlands may be easier for me than home games in many ways but I could do with in-built sat nav.

Tuesday November 27 to Thursday November 29
Rosenborg (away)

I'm working next weekend, which means I have two days off in the week. And what do you do when you have Wednesday and Thursday off work and Chelsea are playing in Norway on the Wednesday night? You go to the game.

I'm travelling out with the club, for the first time. This is my fourth European away and I turned the previous trips, to Stuttgart, Paris and Barcelona, into holidays. But as I'm going to

Trondheim on my day off – as you do – this has to be in and out as quickly as possible.

I have to check in at Gatwick at 4am on Wednesday. I do a full day's work on Tuesday – a 10 hour shift starting at 7am – then head home to wrap up warm before catching the 9pm coach from Birmingham to London. Then it's a train to Gatwick from Victoria.

I reach the airport at about 2am, leaving me an annoying amount of time to kill in the middle of the night. But I'm not alone. As I make my way up the escalator from the platform a man in a Chelsea coat spots my Chelsea scarf and strikes up conversation. He's Michael, from Ilford, a long-term fan who I guess is in his forties. Like me, he's travelling alone and we go for a coffee to pass the time, chatting about previous away trips, favourite players past and present, the managerial situation and all things Chelsea. He's a nice bloke and I'm glad I bumped into him.

Our flight leaves at 6am and the stewardesses are soon apologising for the fact they can't bring us the Transformers Movie as planned. I hope I'll cope. We arrive in Trondheim at about 9.30am, it's freezing and there's thick snow everywhere. This doesn't surprise me – we're in Norway in the winter after all – but it seems to have caught out a number of Blues sporting trainers, brogues and other completely inappropriate footwear, who are sliding about like Torvill and Dean on a bad day.

The coach takes us into town and we're left to our own devices at about 11am – nearly nine hours before kick-off. I've got a guidebook out of the library and know there are a few sights to see. A cathedral, a picturesque river with an island in it, Norway's third-largest art gallery...

But most people just want to get out of the freezing cold. Michael and I join a group trudging through the snow and, both acknowledging the fact that if we start boozing now we could be unconscious and/or bankrupt by kick-off, we go for a coffee. We stay for an hour or so, then head back out into the snow to find somewhere for lunch. Two enormous pizzas later we're back with the "What shall we do now?" dilemma. Deciding you can't come all this way and see nothing of the town we go for a wander for an hour-and-a-half or so, but it's cold enough to make Captain Oates unsure about venturing out and the snow underfoot makes walking quite a challenge, so when we find out what pub people are gathering in we decide to go there.

The Three Lions is, not surprisingly given the name, owned by an Englishman and has Chelsea flags plastered all over it. It's packed to the rafters with Blues fans wrapped up like Nanuk of the North, Blue is the Colour playing loudly and Sky Sports News on the big screen TV. We get a couple of beers and soon realise that the pub may be English-owned but the prices are very much Scandinavian – it works out at £6 a pint. A bit later, needing to kill time, I order something to eat. I'm not really hungry as I'm still digesting the world's largest pizza, so I just go for an omelette. Eleven quid.

We have to catch our bus to the stadium about 90 minutes before kick-off. Among the last to board the coach are two blokes who've clearly been quaffing six quid pints all day. One of them has fallen over, no doubt through a combination of booze and non-sensible shoes, and his friend announces loudly "My mate's broken his collarbone and we've lost Rod Stewart!" The first half of that statement could well be true, but I have no idea about the second bit – though the faux Scotsman behind Sailing and Maggie May is indeed nowhere to be seen, surprisingly.

The Lerkendal Stadion is an average Lego kit 25,000ish-seater stadium, but surrounded by snow-covered slopes it looks surprisingly nice. Also looking surprisingly nice are the stewards searching fans at our entrance – more than half of them are extremely attractive young women. Conditioned by years of knowing that at English grounds men frisk men and women frisk women, I get myself searched by a strapping Viking. Then I watch with dismay as most of the blokes following me head straight for the ladies and, with big grins on their faces, are frisked by them. The lovely ladies, to their credit, appear not to be regarding the visitors as ridiculous sex-pests and are all smiles. Damn. There are few enough chances in this life to be groped by a stunning Scandinavian woman and I've just squandered one of mine. It's a big disappointment.

As with most stadiums, there's music playing before kick-off. But the song played most loudly here is not a Blue is the Colour-style paean to the home team, but a guitar-based ode to the Champions League. How do I know this? Because the only part of the ballad which isn't in Norwegian is the chorus, which goes "Champions League, oh Champions Leeeeeeague..." Who needs Eurovision?

Long sleeves are the order of the day on the pitch and it looks perishing cold out there. Good job they're going to be running about. I'm wearing big walking boots, thick woollen socks, thermal pants, jeans, a thermal vest, my Chelsea shirt, my 1970 FA Cup final replica shirt over that, a big warm winter coat, a scarf, a woolly hat and gloves and I'm not exactly warm. I wouldn't fancy ambling about on the pitch in shirt and shorts.

Of course Rosenborg aren't bad but we dominate the early exchanges and after seven minutes Drogba puts us in front. He celebrates by standing in front of us, pulling an "I'm cold" face, rubbing his hands up and down his chilly arms and pretending to shiver. Say what you like about Drogba, but he's got a sense of humour.

He soon gets his second and Alex makes it 3-0 before half-time with another pile-driving free kick, this one from about 35 yards, flying along just above the ground at about 500mph.

During the break I nip to the gents and spot the two blokes from the coach with a third man who does indeed look like Rod Stewart. It's not him, of course, but at least now I know what they were talking about. If I had a mate who looked like that, I'd call him Rod Stewart too. I'm glad they've been reunited.

In the second half, despite being 3-0 down, the Norwegians continue to make plenty of noise. We serenade them with "You might as well ski home!" Fans in their home end hold up a banner saying "Once we were odd, you still are". Answers on a postcard please. We respond with a chant of "We're so odd it's unbelievable".

Wright-Phillips hits the bar but the fourth goal comes eventually from Joe Cole and it finishes 4-0. We're through to the knockout stages with a game to spare and it's been a cracking performance. The players come over at the end to applaud us for our efforts in the snow and we return the compliment.

We catch the coach back to the airport, where I finally get my chance to be manhandled by a beautiful Norwegian woman when it emerges the area where they search you for bombs, guns and bottles of water is staffed entirely by Nordic goddesses. All good things come to those who wait.

As the flight takes off, we're informed the movie this time will be Mr Bean's Holiday and it's a mere £2.75 for headphones to hear it. Suddenly those six quid pints and £11 omelettes look like bargains. I spurn Rowan Atkinson's darkest hour to get a modicum of sleep before we touch down at Gatwick at about 3.30am. I buy a couple of papers to read the match reports, which are amazingly already in the tabloids, and catch the train to Victoria where Michael and I exchange phone numbers, then go our separate ways. I have to hang around for another hour before catching the 6am coach, which gets stuck in traffic on the M25 while I snooze and reaches Birmingham nearly an hour late.

By the time I get to bed it's 11am on Thursday – a full 53 hours after I last prised myself out of this same bed to go to work on Tuesday. There's devotion for you. But I wouldn't have changed a thing. It's been a fantastic trip.

Chapter 5

Pot noodles and Christmas crackers

Saturday December 1
West Ham (home)

The reason I had two days off for Trondheim was because I'm working this weekend. As we kick off against West Ham today I'm in the office. So be it – it meant I could have the Norway experience, so it's swings and roundabouts. Dad goes to the game in my place, and on my lunch break I head to a nearby pub with my mate Dave to watch some of it on Sky. The main thing that strikes me from the bit I see is that the tackles are flying in. How Luis Boa Morte stays on the pitch is beyond me.

We win 1-0 through a goal from Hammers old boy Joe Cole with 15 minutes left, by which time I'm back at my desk. It's a decent result from a tough game. I speak to dad in the evening and he's enjoyed it too. It's the first game he's been to this season, so I'm glad we won for his sake as well as for the three points. Good stuff.

Saturday December 8
Sunderland (home)

However much you love football, when you have a season ticket and are guaranteed entry to every home league game there are bound to be a couple of matches a year when you wake up feeling obliged to go rather than excited. Sunderland on a cold December afternoon is one of them. If the big clashes with Manchester United, Liverpool or Arsenal, or the eagerly-awaited battles with Spurs or Leeds (Leeds! Remember them?) are a

10-course banquet, Sunderland at home in December is a pot noodle. Sorry, Sunderland fans, it just is.

Managed by Roy 'hard-as-nails-won't-accept-failure' Keane, Sunderland are permanent fixtures in the bottom half without looking enough of a soft touch to go down. We used to swat teams like this aside under Mourinho.

And to be fair, we do today. Drogba is out after a knee operation and while we'll miss him, we have a player as brilliant as Shevchenko to bring in. It annoys me how everyone claims Sheva's been a failure. He scored 14 goals last season – not as many as we hoped for, but hardly Robert Fleck or Chris Sutton. And he gets his fourth of this season to put us ahead today, a cracking diving header. I may be in the minority, but I still think this bloke is class. Though I may not be in the minority, judging by the number of people singing his name. It would be great if he could go on a run of goals and prove he was worth buying after all.

Lamps makes it 2-0 from the spot with 15 minutes left and it's all over. There's just time for Liam Miller to be sent off for Sunderland for pushing Pizarro in the face. His boss will be proud.

A mundane game, mundane opposition, a mundane day really. But three points in the bag with no real problems. A pot noodle – quite filling, reasonably tasty, but very forgettable.

Tuesday December 11
Valencia (home)

When the European draw was made, it looked like this could be a winner-takes-all decider. Instead a combination of our efficiency since that Rosenborg draw and Valencia's surprising incompetence means this is a dead rubber.

But I'm still here for it. I bought my ticket before I knew we'd already be through and to be honest I probably would have come even if I had known. Okay, I boycotted Schalke, but as I said at the time that was only the third European home game I've missed in my lifetime. I've been at all the other 42.

However number 43 is a bit of a damp squib. Nothing to play for doesn't always equal nothing happening, but tonight it has a good go. We're well on top, although the best player on the pitch is Valencia's keeper Santiago Canizares. The man who missed the 2002 World Cup after dropping his aftershave bottle and treading on the broken glass (it's up there with Dave Beasant's salad cream injury isn't it?) is in inspired form and makes a string of great saves. And when Kalou and Joey Cole beat him, their shots come back off the woodwork.

So it's 0-0, we're through as group winners and Valencia are out. Mark brought his girlfriend Anna to the game tonight. Her previous match was the goalless draw with Blackburn. She'll be wondering what all the fuss is about.

Sunday December 16
Arsenal (away)
We didn't lose to Arsenal once under Mourinho but I'm not expecting much out of the game today. Arsenal look far better than they have for three or four years, while we've been quite hit-and-miss under Grant.

Our first trip to the Emirates in May was the day we surrendered our title by only drawing, but we were the better team despite being down to 10 men and it was a performance to be proud of. On top of that I stroked Big Sam on the way out of the ground. Walking away from the stadium with Mark I spotted our big friend/stalking victim standing nearby and tried to give him a quick pat on the arm as I passed. Sadly my hand let me down and it turned into more of a glide down his arm and Mark was in hysterics as he laughed at me, saying: "You stroked Big Sam!"

Today I'm watching at home. My parents like to come up to Birmingham in the pre-Christmas period to enjoy the city's German Market and I've invited them up for the weekend, so we watch the game together in my living room. The first thing of relevance to happen is an injury to our captain. Arsenal's latest 'exuberant tackler' Eboue stamps on Terry's foot in a challenge and JT soon has to go off. Things go from bad to worse in injury time when Cech comes out for a corner but flaps at thin air and William Gallas, of all people, is left with a free header into the net. There couldn't have been a worse scorer than our former hero, the man we loved for years before he demanded a move and announced that if he was ever played for us again he'd score a deliberate own goal.

The second half sees us snap away at Arsenal in more ways than one. Half-chances come and go and tasty tackles fly in. Eboue, the man who crocked John Terry, is stretchered off after a tackle from Joe Cole. Shame.

The game finishes 1-0. A lot of people are saying Grant's done well since taking over and there's no denying we've climbed up the table nor that this is our first defeat since we lost his opening game – two defeats in 18 matches. But you could also say the only times he's had big tests in the league, at Old Trafford and the Emirates, we've been found wanting. We're third, six points adrift of Arsenal. Not good enough.

Wednesday December 19
Liverpool (home)

Liverpool in a cup game – that makes a change. We've got a strong team out for this League Cup quarter-final. Scott Sinclair is out wide, but I'm pleased to see him given a game, and aside of that it's not far off a first choice team. Benitez, of course, needs poking with a stick to take anything but the Champions League seriously and Liverpool have Itandje in goal, someone called Hobbs in defence (his squad number of 46 suggests how close he is to the normal first eleven) and a substitute called Nabil El Zhar. It's not quite Souness, Rush and Dalglish.

Lamps puts us 1-0 up with a shot which deflects deliciously off Carragher, looping over the keeper who can only watch, as helpless as a man who realises he's parked his car on top of a hill with the handbrake off. A minute later Peter Crouch launches a stomach-high tackle on Jon Obi Mikel and is rightly sent off. Ballack comes on for his first appearance since April, which is great news.

We never look likely to surrender the lead and with a minute left Sheva makes it 2-0, sending us all home with huge grins on our faces. Some people play down the Carling Cup these days, but there's no such thing as a nothing game against Liverpool. Their arrogance and whining means you always want to beat them and it's great when you do.

I catch the 11pm coach back to Birmingham, as usual after evening games. It gets me back home at about 2am-ish, depending on the traffic, and I usually listen to the radio while having a bit of a snooze. Tonight at about 1.15am, as we pass through Solihull, BBC Six Music plays terrace favourite The Liquidator. I've never heard it on the radio before. What a great way to finish a fantastic night.

Sunday December 23
Blackburn (away)

I don't know if the fixture computer has a sense of humour, but sending Londoners to deepest Lancashire for a Sunday TV game two days before Christmas suggests it must at least know how to raise a chuckle. I for one won't be heading to Ewood Park. I've never been all that fond of Blackburn but now their coaching staff is awash with Chelsea – Mark Hughes assisted by Eddie Niedzwiecki and Kevin Hitchcock, among others – it's hard to hate them. That's not to say I won't want us to beat them 10-0, mind you.

Of course it's not 10-0. Despite the excitement of the win over Liverpool we aren't playing like world-beaters. We lost our last league game and Blackburn are a good side, so when we finish them off 1-0 thanks to Joe Cole it's a good result. The only pine needle stuck in our Christmassy foot is yet another injury to Petr Cech. Let's hope it's not too bad.

Wednesday December 26
Aston Villa (home)

Santa Claus may be able to travel round the world with a sleigh full of presents on Christmas Eve night, but on Boxing Day I can't even get from Sussex to London. I'm with the family down at my parents' place for the festive season and having seen everyone on Christmas Day, nobody would have objected to me heading to the Bridge today. As I would have done if the public transport system in the South East was any good.

The closest places to my parents' house in Bexhill that will see a train today are Brighton and Tonbridge – both about 30 miles away. There's one National Express coach from Bexhill to London, but it will pull into Victoria just as the half-time whistle blows, so there's not much point. It's a day to wish I had a car, or to accept that sometimes you have to miss a game and if you do, you might as well spend your day being fed and watching Morecambe & Wise.

Our match is on Five Live so I listen to it in the living room and when we go 2-0 down a minute before half-time a part of me is glad I'm not there. The unbeaten home record doesn't look very secure and Lampard has already gone off injured. This is not looking like a happy Christmas for Chelsea. But things begin to improve in injury time when Zat Knight gets sent off for conceding a penalty that Sheva tucks away.

Four minutes after the break, still listening to the commentary as I tuck into another of mum's wonderful Christmas dinners, Sheva cqualises. What a turnaround. And 15 minutes later we're ahead thanks to Alex. But it's not over yet. Villa equalise and then Carvalho gets a red card and suddenly the roast potatoes are under threat of being tainted by the taste of dropped points. Until, that is, Ballack scores an 88th minute free kick – it's a present of three points after all. Or is it? Injury time, Ashley Cole stops the ball on the line with his hand and becomes the third man to be sent off. Gareth Barry sticks the penalty away and suddenly our stocking only has one point in it after all.

It sounds like an amazing game. But it's a win chucked away in injury time, overshadowing the fact it's been an eight-goal thriller and that we've made a decent comeback from 2-0 down. We never get results like this. It's the first time we've let in four goals since Charlton beat us 4-2 on Boxing Day 2003 – four years to the day of course – and our last 4-4 was away to Oxford in March 1988.

Thanks to the British railway system taking Christmas off I haven't even seen it. What a game to miss.

Saturday December 29
Newcastle (home)

After my Boxing Day absence I'm back and there are a few changes on the pitch too. These are not as welcome, though they're mainly caused by injuries and suspensions. Carvalho and Ashley Cole miss out after their red cards and the already-injured Terry, Drogba and Cudicini are joined in the treatment room by Lampard, Shevchenko and Cech. It's a good job we've got a big squad.

I hope these many absences explain the state of our perform-ance today, because we're very poor. Thankfully Newcastle are even worse, but at least they're playing to the best of their lim-ited abilities, something we certainly aren't doing. What chances we create are kept out by the excellent Shay Given until Essien puts us in front after half an hour.

Five minutes after the break Newcastle are level with a goal that sums up how scrappy this match has been. After a mass goalmouth scramble, Nicky Butt prods the ball home from about an inch out. It stays one-all until the 87th minute when a Mikel shot is flicked on by Pizarro to Kalou, who sticks it home from an offside position. The Barcodes go mad but the goal stands.

Three days after conceding four at home, we've needed a late offside winner to see off a poor team from the bottom half of the table. As I leave the ground for the last time in 2007, I can't help thinking how last year we were the best team in the country by a mile, and now we've got this. We may still be third in the table, but we've fallen a long way in a few months. Happy New Year.

Chapter 6

Absent friends

Tuesday January 1
Fulham (away)

What better way to start the New Year than to pop round and visit the neighbours? That's exactly what we're doing with a lunchtime kick-off at Craven Cottage. With QPR the first team to come to the Bridge, in this coming Saturday's cup-tie, it's a proper neighbourly New Year.

I'm not at this game, because I welcomed in 2008 at my desk – working a night shift, finishing at 6am. Us media luvvies have it easy. I just about force myself out of bed and onto the sofa to watch on Sky, never mind making the trek to Putney. Of course Fulham v Chelsea isn't a local derby in the real sense of the term – in the Rangers v Celtic sense of hating each other. But that's not to say we don't want to beat them, for local pride and also because we have to keep up our title challenge, if indeed we're making one. After the loss at Arsenal, dropping points against Villa and the crap display against Newcastle, I'm not so sure.

Fulham are in the bottom three with only two wins all season and have a new boss, international wanderer Roy Hodgson, the man who's seen more of Europe than an Australian with a backpack and a student railcard. Their players certainly seem fired up for their chance to impress Mr Roy. After 10 minutes Moritz Volz bursts into the area and is brought down rashly by Joe Cole. Danny Murphy sticks the penalty away and we're behind.

At Craven Cottage the changing rooms are in a corner on the opposite side of the pitch from the dugouts, which means the second half always gets delayed while one of the managers trudges back to his hutch. Today, as Avram Grant returns after the interval he's pounced on by the Fulham mascot, some sort of badger, who looms as close to our boss as he can without actually touching him. Grant looks like he wants to smack the man in the badger suit but thinks better of it. It might have improved his public standing if he had. The badger v Neil Warnock would be interesting.

Instead Avram's clearly taken out his anger on the players at half-time because they come out looking like a different team. We get a corner, nothing to get excited about with us normally. For all their many and varied wonderful talents, Lamps and Joe have both perfected the art of hitting the first defender with every corner. We just never score from corners.

But when Belletti wins this one, the sense of urgency means he waves away Joe Cole and swings it over himself. And it's a belter. One just like real football teams take, and sometimes score from. Alex heads it back across goal and Kalou heads it in. We've scored from a corner! It's amazing enough that I text Dan and Mark to say "We've got someone who can take corners! Let him take every one!"

The Belletti set-piece magic doesn't stop there. On the hour he swings over a free kick, Clint Dempsey gets a handful of Ballack's shirt and he goes down. Penalty. Ballack gets up to take it himself and we all know Germans don't miss penalties. The turnaround is complete and we win 2-1. The New Year starts with three points and with our game being the early kick-off we are the first winners of 2008.

"Wouldn't it be nice to get on with your neighbours?" sang the Small Faces in their poptabulous 1968 chart smash Lazy Sunday. Personally I find it much nicer to come from 1-0 down to beat them 2-1.

Saturday January 5
Queens Park Rangers (home)

I was really pleased when we drew QPR in the FA Cup. Although, much like with Fulham, it's a bit of a one-sided rivalry (they hate us, we treat them like a little brother) it's a shame we haven't played them for so long. In the 12 years since we last did, we've played Barcelona eight times. If there's one statistic that shows how much football – and Chelsea – has changed, I guess that's it.

Right now they're near the bottom of the Championship, so we ought to see them off without much trouble. But then again, we've got half our team missing, haven't been playing well lately and Rangers' form has improved a lot. And they should have the support of a few thousand noisy fans who hate us and have been waiting since 1996 for even a glimmer of a chance to put one over on us.

When I reach the ground there are police and stewards everywhere - more than I can ever remember seeing at a game. I have a bag with me, which means for the first time ever I get searched by a sniffer dog on the way in. What are they expecting to find?

Ballack is on the bench, meaning skipper today is Ashley Cole. He just doesn't seem like a Chelsea captain to me, and I'm sure I'm not alone in thinking that. It soon becomes obvious why QPR are near the bottom of the Championship; they aren't very good. They hardly get near our goal in the first half and we take the lead just before the half-hour. Pizarro, who again looks a bit off the pace, hits a shot from just outside the area which takes an age to go into the net. When the replay comes up on the screen it's clear why. Pizarro's shot hit the post, bounced out, hit the goalkeeper on the back and trickled over the line. It won't win goal of the season and it's an own goal, so despite Pizarro accepting the acclaim of the crowd and his team-mates, he still hasn't scored since the opening day.

In the second half Drogba comes on, just in time to leave for the African Cup of Nations, but it's still good to have him back. He takes the captain's armband from Cole, making him the sixth man to wear it in three weeks after Terry, Lampard, Ballack and the two Coles. Who'll be next, I wonder?

Although QPR put up more of a challenge towards the end, they never look like scoring and we rarely look like adding to the fortunate goal. And disappointingly the atmosphere is surprisingly flat, with both sets of fans quieter than I expected. So, after 12 years of waiting to renew the rivalry, instead of a highly charged local derby cup tie, we get a bit of a damp squib. I was hoping for more.

Tuesday January 8
Everton (home)

Our reward for beating Liverpool in the quarter-finals of the Carling Cup is the chance to beat the blue half of Merseyside in the semis. I used to hate Everton as a boy. When I was eight they played Watford in the 1984 FA Cup final. Although Chelsea got promoted that year the prospect of us ever being in a big game like the cup final seemed so alien to me that I regarded it as a proper special occasion, like cup finals should be, and I wanted Watford to win. They were the underdogs, so I kept hearing. But their chairman was Elton John, a man I was well aware of thanks to years of exposure to Radio Two at home. The idea that a team led by the man who sang Goodbye Yellow Brick Road could somehow be inferior to Everton, about whom I knew very little, puzzled me.

But Everton won 2-0 and it was made worse by the fact the second goal was a clear foul by Andy Gray on Steve Sherwood in the Watford goal. I was not happy. If I'd known then that Sherwood was an ex-Chelsea player it might have been too much to take. Instead I developed a loathing of Everton – and Andy Gray – that lasted about five years. In that time they won the league twice, reached two more cup finals and won the Cup Winners' Cup. I must have been furious.

After hating Everton in the mid-80s, I've since grown to realise they tend to be the acceptable face of Merseyside football. A couple of good mates are Everton fans and on the rare occasions you meet a quiet, shy and self-effacing Scouser who didn't go to school with John Lennon and knock Jimmy Tarbuck's tooth sideways, they're usually Evertonians.

Amazingly, this is Everton's first major semi in 13 years. In that time we've had 17, plus another the year before for good measure. No wonder I don't hate them like I used to. Elton John and Steve Sherwood must be easing off on the voodoo dolls as well.

As the game starts it soon becomes clear tonight's ref is quite fond of Everton, as they get every decision going. Phil Neville makes at least four bookable challenges and only gets a yellow card for one of them. Despite this Wright-Phillips, in central midfield as we're so short, puts us in front with a cracking goal and we're playing very well. We boss the rest of the half and look most likely to score again, but reach the break 1-0 up.

Ten minutes into the second half though, the ref strikes. John Obi Mikel fouls Teflon Man Neville, a yellow card offence I'd say. Out comes the red. Mikel trudges off disconsolately, but knowing he shouldn't have gone we applaud him off and he waves to all sides of the ground. It's his last game before the African Cup of Nations and he's arguably been our best player so far this season. He'll serve his suspension while unavailable anyway with his Nigeria commitments, but it doesn't alter the fact we have to play 35 minutes tonight with 10 men.

We weather the storm for 10 minutes until Everton are gifted a mystery free-kick. Two players go up for a header, nobody touches anyone and somehow it's a foul. McFadden swings the ball into our area. It's cleared but Yobo hooks it back in and Yakubu fires a fantastic shot into the back of the net. Thanks ref. And we've got 25 minutes of this left. Minutes later McFadden hits the far post and we really are hanging on.

As we get into injury time I'm begging for the final whistle but we mount one last attack and, amazingly, Wright-Phillips, the shortest man on the pitch, leaps up to head the ball into the net. It later emerges he didn't – although he outjumped the much taller Lescott, it was the Everton defender who headed the ball into the net. Shaun may not have scored two after all then, but he's been fantastic. If he played this well on a regular basis he'd be a star.

But the real story tonight is of a remarkable win against the odds. Our 10 men beat their 12.

Saturday January 12
Tottenham Hotspur (home)

Spurs. Ask any proper Chelsea fan what teams they hate and what matches they look forward to and Tottenham will be high on both lists. There isn't a game that goes by where we don't at some point sing songs about Tottenham, whether it be the simple warning to them that they should "surrender or you'll die", the announcement that "North London is full of shit", or a far more elaborate tale of a Papal decree that the "boys in blue and white" are "the team we all adore".

Of course Tottenham are traditionally the club favoured by London's Jewish community and while there may have been an anti-Semitic nature to some of the hatred way back, that's never been an issue for me and I honestly don't think it is for 99% of fans. We just hate Tottenham because they are, well, Tottenham.

Growing up in north-east London in the early eighties, there were loads of Tottenham fans at my primary school. Spurs and Liverpool were the teams to support. Liverpool were England's most successful club, winning European Cups and countless league titles, while Tottenham were the most successful and glamorous London club. It sounds laughable now, but they were a big deal. The sad thing is most Spurs fans think they still are, and always have been.

Tottenham were rarely out of the bottom half of the league in the 1990s. Yet I knew Spurs fans who would have displayed major disappointment if the Brazil 1970 team had turned up at their peak and Spurs had only beaten them 1-0. Over the past few years, when we went an incredible 32 league games against them unbeaten and while we've been picking up trophy after trophy and Spurs have been picking up the odd point here and there, I've often thought back to those days when Spurs fans used to ask me "Why do you support Chelsea? They're rubbish!" Now they know why. Or not, because the self-delusion rampant at White Hart Lane manifests itself in the belief that theirs is football of the utmost purity and winning would somehow dilute this.

Two years ago, level at 1-1 at home to Spurs in injury time, William Gallas picked up the ball out on the left wing, cut inside and hammered the ball into the top corner from about 25 yards. It remains one of the most incredible moments I've experienced at Stamford Bridge. We went berserk and the revelry continued in the pub, where Dan was in such celebratory mood he ordered a bottle of champagne. By the time I decided to go home I'd missed my coach but managed to drunkenly talk the driver of a later coach into letting me on. Either that or he was just so keen for our conversation to end he ushered me onto the bus. Once on board I got my coat stuck to a seat and ripped a big hole in it. I won the game but lost a coat.

So will there be such fun and games today? We've won four in a row since drawing with Villa, but they've all been unconvincing. Spurs are in the bottom half although they've picked up a bit lately. New boy Nicolas Anelka, signed yesterday for £15 million, is on the bench and Cech is back in goal, though we still have half the team missing. I'd take any sort of win today.

The game starts scrappily and nothing of real note happens until a moment of genuine brilliance after 20 minutes. Belletti gets the ball just inside their half, takes a couple of strides forward then blasts a shot that goes like the straightest and truest of arrows right into the top corner of Radek Cerny's net. It was one of those where you can tell its destination from the second the ball leaves the player's foot. In the Matthew Harding Stand we were 100 yards away but directly in line with the ball as it flew through the air and into the net. It was a glorious goal and if we score a better one this season I'll be amazed. We always seem to have memorable moments when Spurs come to town.

Anelka comes on after the break for Pizarro, who has again been poor. He gets a great reception and almost scores with his first touch. Spurs pose little threat and a second goal from Wright-Phillips kills the game off. There's still time for another chance for Anelka, who hits the bar. It's a shame, we were all willing that one to go in to make a good day great.

It's been a very straightforward win, a lot easier than expected. Against different opposition this would have felt quite run-of-the-mill, but there's no such thing against Tottenham. Any win against our old rivals is always good.

Saturday January 19
Birmingham City (away)

Another away game in Birmingham and another stadium I can walk to. So of course again I get on the tram to West Bromwich and meet Chris and John at the Hind. The pub is full of West Brom fans, as you'd expect, because they're at home to Cardiff. When I see the length of the queue for food, I decide to just have a beer. After the shouted-at-for eating curry from-a-saucepan-with-chip-forks incident last time, perhaps it's for the best.

The visit to the pub is incident free but, after currygate and the Derby pub confusion, if it's an away game in the Midlands there has to be a bizarre moment. This time it comes after Chris has driven us back into Birmingham and parked near the ground. A man who sees him park his Volvo stops us and asks if we would like to buy another Volvo from him. He's obviously working on the basis that you can never have too many Volvos.

The man shows us the car in question and Chris, to his great credit, humours him all the way, pretending to be interested, until the would-be vendor makes the mistake of saying "And there's a baby seat in the back". Chris points at John, his 6ft-plus 23-year-old medical student son, and shouts: "Baby seat? This is my baby! I don't need a baby seat!" We leave and make our way to the ground.

Anelka is making his first start but there's still no Terry or Lampard, as well as all the African players. We dominate possession but aren't playing well and our cause isn't helped when Shaun Wright-Phillips, who's been in great form lately, has to go off. Pizarro, without a goal since we played this lot on the first day of the season, comes on. Petr Cech makes a good attempt at creating the most embarrassing goal of the season by dilly-dallying with the ball at his feet and slicing a clearance straight to Birmingham's Cameron Jerome, who heads the ball against the post. A very lucky escape.

In the second half Birmingham have two more very good chances but with 10 minutes left, Juliano Belletti, the man who can take corners, swings one over and Pizarro, of all people, guides a great acrobatic diving header through a crowd and into the net. We win 1-0. It's the sixth win in a row but we haven't played well.

Man United and Arsenal have also won, so we remain four points behind the pair of them – well in touch. As we walk off in the pouring rain back to Chris's car, he declares "If we win the Premier League, the rest of the Premier League should hang their heads in shame." Despite the fact we've just taken three points away to a team who drew at Arsenal last week, it's hard to disagree.

Wednesday January 23
Everton (away)

Tottenham hammered Arsenal 5-1 in the second leg of the other semi last night, so we're fighting for the right to meet our traditional London rivals in a Wembley final for the first time since 1967. But first we have to defend a one-goal lead against a good Everton side. Michael Ballack has joined the list of missing players, meaning Claude Makelele becomes our seventh captain in five weeks and Steve Sidwell gets another opportunity in midfield. There were people who thought he'd never get a game for us when he signed, but with our injuries this is his 23rd of the season.

I'm at work until 8pm, which is kick-off time, so I listen to the first 15 minutes on the radio as I rush home, before settling down to watch the rest on Sky. We start the game on the back foot but for all Everton's possession they don't really trouble Petr Cech and we soak up the pressure. In the second half we look more of a threat and Anelka hits the bar. It's his third game for us and he has already hit the bar twice but not scored. I hope it's not a sign of things to come.

With about 20 minutes left Malouda plays a good long ball to Joe Cole, who brings it down fantastically and hits a great shot past Tim Howard. It's a fabulous bit of skill and enough to kill Everton off. Over 180 minutes it's been a tough test and we've come through it well to reach yet another cup final. I'm delighted and very much looking forward to a final against Spurs next month. I won't be watching that one on the telly.

Saturday January 26
Wigan (away)
Another away cup tie in the North West, another I'm watching on TV. When the BBC announced this would be the Saturday teatime game for the FA Cup fourth round, I decided saving money and watching it at home was probably the way forward. And I'm glad I did because I'm full of cold and glad not to have to go out.

I'm not alone in watching with Messrs Lineker, Hansen et al. Wigan never get decent crowds and there are only 14,000 there tonight. We nearly score in the opening minute, but Joe Cole puts his shot wide and we reach half-time goalless.

After the break a through ball from Juliano Belletti for Anelka to chase looks over-hit, but our £15 million man stretches out a leg and prods the ball over Chris Kirkland as he rushes out. Account opened, and hopefully the first of many. Wigan appeal for offside, but it isn't.

With eight minutes left Wright-Phillips puts us 2-0 up with his third goal in three weeks and it looks over. But it's rarely that simple these days and Wigan sub Sibierski makes it 2-1. Inevitably they throw everything at us and Marcus Bent hits the bar in stoppage time, but we hold on and reach round five. It's been tough at the end however we're through. Lemsip? Tunes? No, I'll treat my cold with the warm glow that comes from an away win in the FA Cup.

Wednesday January 30
Reading (home)

This is the first time I've ever seen us play Reading. I missed the home game last year because it was on Boxing Day and I had family commitments (and probably wouldn't have been able to get to it anyway). So Reading at home on a cold Wednesday evening in January holds more interest for me than many people. For most the main attraction is the chance to boo Stephen Hunt for his awful challenge on Petr Cech last year, when he fractured our keeper's skull. I'll be happy to join in with that. And he does indeed get an awful barracking every time he touches the ball.

Ballack gets on the end of a great cross from Paulo Ferreira and heads home brilliantly for the only goal of the game. Thank God he's come back to fitness just as Lampard and Essien have been out. Without him we'd have been really struggling in midfield lately.

Amazingly, we haven't lost since John Terry got injured at Arsenal and we've won every game since Lampard and Shevchenko went off injured against Villa. These nine wins in a row equal the best run in our 103-year history. To do it without Terry, Lampard, Essien, Drogba, Mikel, Kalou and Shevchenko, plus Carvalho serving a three-match suspension, is little short of astounding. Is Avram Grant a managerial genius after all, or are our reserves (if it's fair to dub Ballack, Makelele, Alex, Anelka et al as such) playing out of their skins because they see this is a chance to shine?

Either way, whisper it quietly but we're the form team in the Premier League. Four points off the top with a load of stars to come back and boost our squad. Doesn't look bad, does it?

I get home at 2am and have to be at work for 10. Given we were only playing Reading, maybe some people would have missed it. But I saw us make history (or at least equal it). Who needs eight hours sleep?

Chapter 7

Pimps and Parthenons

Saturday February 2
Portsmouth (away)

Despite getting rid of Jose Mourinho and replacing him with Avram Grant and despite nearly all our best players being injured or away in Africa, we're in with a chance of setting a new club record for consecutive wins. But it's far from a foregone conclusion. Pompey are good and our run surely has to end sometime, given we've been grinding out results with a patched-up team.

I'm not at the game, again. It's a long way from Birmingham to Portsmouth and I'm in the middle of a run of night shifts, so I enjoy it in the company of Jeff Stelling and co on Sky rather than John Portsmouth Football Club Nelson Mary Rose, or whatever his name is, and that bell of his. The first half seems tight and ends 0-0 but 10 minutes after the break we're in front. What sounds like a cracking passing move ends with Anelka volleying home Joe Cole's lay-off for his first league goal for us.

Could we really be about to get our 10th win in a row, in a run in which Terry, Lampard, Drogba, Shevchenko and Essien have played three games between them? The answer is no. Jermain Defoe signed for Portsmouth from Tottenham right on the transfer deadline so he has to score. 1-1.

All good things must come to an end and it's hardly a surprise that our team, half made-up of reserves since Christmas, should stop winning some time. It's obviously disappointing not to break the record, but it shouldn't obscure the fact that, under the injury and Africa-hit circumstances, this is a good away point.

Sunday February 10
Liverpool (home)

The day starts well. The talking point from the Manchester derby, two-and-a-half hours before our game, should have been the minute's silence for the 50th anniversary of the Munich crash being impeccably observed (What's that? Football fans not behaving like barbarians? Surely not!). Instead the talking point becomes City winning. The last season they won at Old Trafford, United got relegated. Hopefully it's an omen, but I won't hold my breath.

It means if we beat Liverpool we'll go level on points with United, who a lot of people make favourites for the title even though Arsenal are top with a game in hand. Instead we turn in one of our worst performances for a long time.

Lampard is back for the first time since Boxing Day, which is great, but looks unfit. Nobody in midfield seems to be able to pass to a blue shirt. Anelka is totally isolated up front and spends too much time on the wing. If we were playing a decent team in good form we'd have lost, but thankfully Liverpool are almost as bad as us. It finishes 0-0 and is one of the dullest, matches seen at the Bridge for a very long time. Ashley Cole is our best player by a mile (yes really) and about the only one to emerge with any credit.

If Arsenal win at home tomorrow night they'll be eight points clear of us. I can't see us making that up.

Saturday February 16
Huddersfield Town (home)

The last 16 of the FA Cup and we're at home to League One opposition. You can't grumble with that. I'm off to Athens on Monday morning for the Olympiacos game and could do with saving a bit of money so I miss this one and follow it at home.

Out-of-town gloryhunting armchair fans are ruining the game.

After Lampard's return last weekend, Terry is back today, for the first time since he had his foot broken by Eboue at Arsenal. It's great timing – our reserves got a load of wins in January but they've started to look tired. Today also sees the return of some of our African stars, with Kalou and Mikel starting and Essien on the bench, as is Sheva, fit for the first time since Boxing Day. That's a lot of quality to have back at once.

We go in front on 18 minutes, when Scott Sinclair sets up Lamps for his 100th Chelsea goal, an incredible achievement for a midfielder. He's been an absolutely wonderful player for us. A hundred goals in less than seven years would be brilliant on its own, but he's also a great passer of the ball, fantastically consistent, gives everything for the cause, has more skill than many people give him credit for, takes a reliable penalty, fulfils his defensive duties and grabs games by the scruff of the neck. This is also a man England fans boo when he plays for the national team.

We look like we're getting to half-time with a narrow lead when suddenly, from nowhere, Huddersfield equalise right on the whistle. Hmm. But in the second half the ever-dependable Frank gets goal number 101, then Kalou makes it 3-1 and it's game over.

So we're into the last eight. But Liverpool aren't. Amazingly they lose 2-1 at home to Barnsley. Barnsley! Phil Thompson's face on Sky is absolutely hilarious. When Barnsley – Barnsley!! – get their last minute winner he looks like he might explode. In the evening kick-off Man United beat Arsenal 4-0 in a game so one-sided it's embarrassing. It's opening up very nicely – and of course we're also in the Carling Cup final. This could turn out to be quite some season. I have to admit I didn't think it would.

Monday February 18

I'm getting good at this coach-down-the-motorway-in-the-mid-dle-of-the-night lark. This time it's the 4.15am service from

Birmingham to Heathrow, ready for my early morning flight to Athens. When we got drawn against Olympiacos in December I booked flights and a hotel within four hours of the balls coming out of the bag, or hat, or bowl, or whatever they use at Uefa Towers.

The cheapest flight I could get was with Lufthansa and involves changing planes in Munich. When I get to Germany I find the flight to Athens is delayed because of heavy snow in Athens. Heavy snow in Athens? When is there ever heavy snow in Athens? I'd checked the weather forecast and knew it had been cold there and even that there might be a light sprinkling of snow, but heavy snow?

When we take off I'm sat next to a woman from Athens, who must be about 40. As we come in to land she leans across me to watch her city covered in snow, because she's never seen it like this before. My trip to Athens has coincided with the heaviest snowfall there in decades.

Tuesday February 19
Olympiacos (away)

The sun's out and the snow's melting. But it's a slow process and good fun to watch the Athenians try to cope, because they don't have any experience of it. Shops have crowds of men outside trying to clear pavements even the English would manage to have snowless with one tub of salt.

I head for the Acropolis and it's quite a treacherous journey, at the top of a hill best accessed via some side streets and steep steps covered in melting snow and sheet ice. I'm as surefooted as Arjen Robben in a 'fool the ref into thinking you've been fouled' competition.

The Acropolis is amazing. It's incredible to think these pieces of marble have been there for thousands of years and were once walked around by the likes of Socrates – the Greek philosopher, not the 1980s Brazilian midfielder. Although billions of people will have been here over the years, I'm one of the few to see the

Parthenon and its neighbours covered in both snow and Chelsea fans.

I chat to some fellow travellers about disrupted flights. I got off very lightly, some were diverted to Rhodes for 24 hours. And I gather that people are generally heading for Syntagma Square, the main square in the city centre, which is surrounded by bars and also home to the parliament building.

So later in the afternoon I head there. Some people I know were supposed to be coming out for the day and this is probably my best chance of finding them, and even if I don't I'll be able to mingle with some like-minded Blues fans. When I reach the square a short man, probably in his 50s, speaks to me in Greek. When I tell him I don't understand he says "Ah you are English! Here for the football? I know England very well. My wife is from Sheffield in South Yorkshire." His geographical attention to detail puts me at ease.

"We run an English bar on the corner," he continues. "Come and have a drink." My first instinct is no, but I think about how a) it's common practice for bars on the continent to employ people to stand outside to try to drag punters in; and b) if he does run an English bar on the square where all the Chelsea fans are supposedly gathering, it will be full of Chelsea.

So I go with him. I've come out here on my own and perhaps it's time to stop being a Billy-No-Mates. We chat as we walk, and he asks me where in Greece I've been before and what other countries I've been to with Chelsea. But I begin to get concerned about how far we're walking and ask where his bar is. He replies "You English, you are so suspicious. It's just up here."

We turn into a quiet street and I realise he's walking in front of me, another man is right behind me and another is on my left, walking in the road. I'm surrounded and fairly sure by now there is no bar and I'm about to get jumped on and robbed, beaten up or worse. "Where's this bar then?" I ask again. "Just here" he replies, opening the door to what is indeed a bar. As I make my way in I expect the two henchmen to follow me but they just walk past. Looks like I was worrying about nothing.

He tells me to sit at the bar and instructs his barmaid to pour me a beer. I take a seat and soon realise this "English pub" is about as English as moussaka and there's hardly anyone here – just a handful of old blokes at the bar. So I tell him I'll just stay for one drink. He beckons his barmaid round to our side of the bar, introduces her as Svetlana, from Russia, and tells her to sit next to me. She asks my name and when I say it's James her eyes light up and she says "Like James Bond?" Her next line is "You buy me a drink?" and, not knowing what else to do, I say yes. One of the cronies goes behind the bar, produces what appears to be a bottle of champagne and pours Svetlana a glass. So it's one of those kind of bars. It might have been cheaper getting mugged.

I have no plans to stay any longer than I need to, my wallet might not take it, and I don't feel safe. Svetlana makes small talk while I try to drink as quickly as possible. The bloke who got me in here leans over and says "You and the girl can go somewhere more comfortable?" So it really is one of those bars. I reply "No, here at the bar is just fine." For the second time he says "You English..."

I may be wolfing my drink down as quickly as I can, but I can't match the pace of Svetlana, who must be very thirsty. I'm barely halfway through mine when she finishes hers and asks for another. When I say no, she begins to demand rather than ask. I am told, "You buy me another drink!" four or five times, but each time I say no, realising I need to get increasingly firm. With my answers, that is.

She finally gets the hint and says "So you just want the cheque?" and I say yes. Blokey behind the bar grins and gets out a receipt pad. Five Euros for my beer, 30 Euros for Svetlana's champagne/grape juice/whatever it was. To be honest I've got off lightly. I pay up and say my goodbyes.

I leave the bar and make sure I've got my wallet, passport, camera, mobile phone, watch and health. All intact. Maybe I was very naïve to go with the bloke in the first place? Maybe I completely over-reacted? Maybe some people in my shoes would have stayed a while, gone "somewhere comfortable", had a great time and come out with a smile on their face? Well, I didn't feel comfortable. I was tricked in there in the first place, which I don't like, and – call me a big girl if you want – I didn't come to Athens to visit knocking shops. I head back to my hotel feeling a bit chastened.

Of course, Russian prostitutes aside, this is a match day. So I'm back out in the evening to catch the metro to Piraeus, home of Olympiacos. There are plenty of Blues about, including various faces I recognise from away games. A slightly odd Olympiacos fan mingles with us on the journey and tells us we're going to lose 5-0.

When we get to the stadium I attempt to get something to eat and find a stall selling enormous baguettes with sausages or chips. But it soon becomes clear that "or" is not an option. Being a vegetarian, I ask for some chips in mine, no sausage. The woman tells me I can't have that. I tell her I'll pay full price, for sausage, chips and bread, but I just don't want a sausage. "No," she tells me. "Why not? I'll pay for all of it. I will pay you full price and be taking less food," I try to explain. She glares at me and calls out to a big man standing nearby. I don't know whether he's her boss, an undercover cop or just some heavy who prevents vegetarians getting a decent meal, but I'm not staying around to find out. After the day I've had, the last thing I want is to get beaten up or arrested in an argument about sausages. I clear off and make do with a bag of crisps for my dinner. With this and the West Bromwich curry, what is it with me and vegetarianism in foreign lands?

There are huge nets between the fans and the pitch on three sides of the stadium. It's obviously only the people in the posh seats they trust not to throw things at the players. Looking at the number of flares being set off in the away end, maybe they've got a point.

After the 'odd' banner in Trondheim, tonight's mystery message from the home fans is "Byron fanatic". I'm no philistine – I enjoy Lines Inscribed Upon a Cup Formed From a Skull as much as the next man. But a fanatic? Each to his own.

Terry and Lampard are on the bench, which doesn't go down well. They've both been injured, the team did well without them and we've got a cup final in five days time, but they aren't the sort of players who welcome a rest nor the sort of players we can readily do without in our team.

Olympiacos are solid but unspectacular. Midfielder Stoltidis looks their best player, while Djordjevic and Galletti are also lively. Our best chances in the first half are from a Carvalho header and a decent shot from Malouda, which their goalkeeper Nikopolidis, the one who looks like George Clooney, deals with fairly comfortably.

It's still cold and there's snow on the sidelines. Drogba, recently back from Africa, doesn't look like he's having fun. After the break we liven up a bit without ever really looking convincing. Anelka, Kalou and Lampard come on and Kalou has the best chance of the match in extra time, but his control lets him down and his shot is weak. It finishes 0-0.

Not a bad result on the face of it. We need to win at home but we should do; Olympiacos are nothing special. I'm happy with the result even if it hasn't been a great game to travel all this way for.

Throughout the match the home fans closest to us have pelted us with coins. Our stock response has been to chant the name of their greatest rivals, Panathinaikos, which does not go down well. After the final whistle, they up the ante a bit. Bottles and cans are added to the coins flying into our section. A full can of beer misses me by inches. The police won't let us out until all the home fans have gone but the cops seem as interested in making them leave as they are in stopping them chucking stuff at us, namely not at all. We're English hooligans and deserve no less.

With the two-hour time difference, it's gone 11.30pm when the game ends. By the time the missiles run out, the home fans clear off and we finally get out, it's a quarter past midnight.

The metro back into the city is only calling at one stop, much to the dismay of most people. Thankfully for me it's Omonia, the station round the corner from my hotel. We get there about 12.50am. Some people look round for taxis back to their hotel, others look for bars. I grab a slice of spinach pie from the take-away on the corner and head back to my hotel.

It's nearly 1am and I've been bombarded with coins, beer cans and prostitutes. It's time to call it a night.

Wednesday February 20

I'm not leaving Athens until tomorrow, so I've got a day sight-seeing. And I have a nice day, strolling through a big park and visiting the stadium used for the 1896 Olympics, among other things.

Then, at about 5.30pm, I'm taking a photo of the Temple of Zeus when a man gets up from a bench where he was sitting with a friend and says "You were in our bar yesterday!" It's the bloke who smiled with glee when he handed me the bill for Svetlana's drink. I could believe it if I was near the bar, but I'm a good 20 minutes walk away, in a different direction from the square where I got collared yesterday.

I try to ignore him but he won't let me. "Yes, you came in our bar and you had one drink! One drink!" He's not going to go away, so I reply. "Oh yeah, I did..." And he says, "Come to our bar. Come back to our bar today!"

There's no chance I'm going there ever again so I tell him no thanks and walk off. "You come to our bar!" he shouts. Persistent, I'll give him that.

Five minutes later I'm taking a photo of what's left of some other ancient marble structure just round the corner, when I hear a voice shouting "Hey!" I look round and it's the other bloke, the one who stayed on the bench while his mate mocked me. I've had enough of this now so I walk off, fairly quickly.

He's still shouting "Hey, hey" so I look round again and find the man, who must be in his 60s, running across the road, still shouting and now waving his fist at me. He is actually chasing me. As he crosses the road I nip back across to where he's come from. He comes back over so I cross again, always about five yards up the road from him. He follows me again, so I cross again. He's genuinely chasing me, cat-and-mouse-style, as we both zig-zag across the road.

I was prepared to accept I brought yesterday's events upon myself by going to the 'English bar'. Bumping into the barman again today was such a coincidence it brought a smile to my face. But this is too much. I'm being chased up the road by an elderly pimp, waving his fists at me.

There are other people about, presumably wondering what on earth I've done to this poor old man. And to make it all the more bizarre, the whole episode is happening in the shadow of the Temple of Zeus, built by Emperor Hadrian, him with the wall, nearly 2,000 years ago. What would Hadrian and Zeus make of this?

There's a metro station just down the road, so I jog there. The bloke gives up, still shouting, and I get a train back to my hotel. No doubt I'll soon be seeing the funny side of this and it will be a story I enjoy telling time and time again in the pub after I get back to England. But right now I've had enough of Athens, pimps, prostitutes, English bars and old blokes.

Sunday February 24
Tottenham Hotspur (Wembley)

When Chelsea reached our first cup final in my lifetime I was 18. Three years later I was at Wembley when we won our first trophy in my lifetime, the 1997 FA Cup. Just being in finals felt amazing in those days, but since then we've barely been out of them. And I realise how lucky I am to be supporting a team enjoying such success.

It's still less than a year since the new Wembley opened and this Carling Cup final is already our third trip here. Arsenal and Liverpool are both still waiting for their first. Before the FA Cup final last May I was here before midday. I had a nose around and then met up with Dan, Chris and John for a few beers. I attempt to do the same today, but not having arranged anything in advance, it's a case of texting to see who's around. And nobody is. John replies that he's been unexpectedly delayed by being unable to get his bike on the train and suddenly I feel I've been transported back to the 1950s when players and fans travelled to the game together by bus and people, er, couldn't fit their bike on the train.

When I take my seat in the stadium I find out Joe Cole is only on the bench. What's Grant thinking of? Joe's been in great form lately, at his creative best, playing a key role in that great run of wins in January. Apart from being rested for the Huddersfield match he hasn't missed a game since November. And what's his reward for this excellent run of consistency and quality? To be left out of the team for a cup final. He must be gutted.

It's not just harsh on him – it's a downright bad decision. His replacement on the wing is Nicolas Anelka and it smacks of Grant knowing he has to play Drogba, but also feeling obliged to play the man he's paid £15 million for. Wright-Phillips is on the other wing and while he's played well lately, I'd never pick him ahead of Cole, and especially not for a game like this. Ballack is also left out, which I'm not sure is wise.

With this being a cup final they have to do things a bit differently. When the teams are announced, the reading of each name is accompanied by someone carrying a huge flag bearing that name, marching out into something close to their position on the pitch. Once all 22 are out there the flag-bearers dance around in clever formation to the tune of Great DJ by the Ting-Tings. Hark at me, I'm 32 and I can still recognise songs from the hit parade.

How would someone get a job like that? Maybe you wander into the job centre and there's a card on the wall saying "Person wanted to prance around hallowed turf carrying an enormous flag with WRIGHT-PHILLIPS written on it. Similar vacancy for a ZOKORA."

The match doesn't start well. Spurs look more up for it and, frankly, better. They almost take the lead inside the first minute when Terry has to divert Robbie Keane's shot away from goal. Our team is every bit as unbalanced as I feared. Anelka looks like he's sulking on the wing and on the other side Wright-Phillips has put the good form of the past few weeks behind him and reverted to type; misplaced passes, awful crosses that fly out of play, scared to take defenders on, vanishing for long periods. Would Joe Cole really have been no better?

After about 20 minutes I realise we haven't had a shot. The bloke next to me is looking up something in his programme so I ask him if it says in there what time we'll get our first shot at goal. When it finally happens, he and I turn to each other and say "28 minutes!" We're in a cup final and there's nearly half an hour gone before we get a shot at goal. How awful is that?

But soon after that they give away a free-kick in a dangerous area and Drogba curls it around the wall and past Robinson. Suddenly all is right with the world. All the noise is from our end and the Spurs fans are silenced. Drogba scored both our goals when we came from behind to beat Arsenal in last year's final, he got the only goal in the FA Cup final and he's opened the scoring today. That means he's scored four consecutive goals in the major domestic cup finals. If anyone's ever matched that, I'll be astounded. He really is the man for the big occasion.

The goal seems to knock the wind out of Tottenham's sails and after bossing most of the first half they are more subdued now. But while we don't look like surrendering the lead we also don't look like adding to it.

Then with about 20 minutes left Wayne Bridge blocks an innocuous cross and suddenly the linesman is flagging furiously. The ref looks over and gives a penalty. I don't believe it. Apparently it was handball, not that the referee saw it . It seems very harsh.

Cech is a great goalkeeper but never stops penalties. And he doesn't stop this one from Berbatov. We haven't played well and probably don't deserve to be in front, but this is a bad way to lose the lead. Ballack finally comes on with two minutes to go, although there's still no Joe Cole. We sing his name over and over to make our views clear, but it falls on Grant's deaf ears.

Even when we enter extra time Cole isn't on. And we're soon behind. Jenas crosses from a free kick, Cech comes out but punches the ball against Woodgate's face. It loops back over him in slow motion and finally bounces into the net. A lucky goal, but we've been asking for it. Joe finally gets brought on after 98 minutes. He inevitably livens the team up, but it's to no avail. We have a couple of good chances near the end through Cole and Kalou, but the ball won't go in. We lose 2-1 and we deserve to.

On the way down I never dreamt we'd lose. We don't lose to Tottenham. And under Jose we didn't lose big games like this. But Jose isn't here anymore and Grant's tactical shortcomings were shown up badly today. He got the team selection wrong and took far too long to realise it. Players were played out of position, some were kept on when they were playing badly. It's hard not to think this would never have happened under Jose.

This has been such a bad day. Can we have a proper manager now please?

Chapter 8

Bothered by Barnsley

Saturday March 1
West Ham (away)

I never seem to be able to go to West Ham. The last time I did Mark Stein scored the winner, so that shows how long ago it was.

Two years ago tickets sold out before I even logged on to the website to buy one, last year I couldn't go after the game got moved to a Wednesday night and today I'm at work. So be it. I'd like to be there but after last weekend's debacle I can live with missing out.

I'm on my lunch break when the match starts and return to my desk at about quarter past three. I find out it's 0-0. But within a minute we've taken the lead and five minutes later we're 3-0 up. What a difference a week makes. Lampard, Joe Cole and Ballack score and it sounds like we're absolutely rampant. Then Frank gets sent off, harshly by the sound of it. Down to 10 men, surely the wheels can't come off badly enough that we surrender a three goal lead?

They don't. Ashley Cole gets his first goal for us and we win 4-0. Away from home, with 10 men. That's some reaction to the Wembley horror show. I may not have been at Upton Park but several of my Stamford Bridge neighbours were, lapping it up. John texts me after the final whistle saying: "M8.u need to watch motd 2nit.its like mourinho was manager.best team in London."

Hi prs indd.

Wednesday March 5
Olympiacos (home)

I prepared for the Olympiacos away game with a trip to the Acropolis. I prepare for today's home leg with a trip to The Fresh Pizza Company at Victoria station. More fattening but less snow.

On taking my seat it's pretty clear that yet again the European night hasn't tempted many of my mates. There are strangers all around, except for two pleasant blokes who sit in the row in front, who I often speak to but whose names I don't even know. One of them turns to me and says, "We're the loyal fans, eh?"

Greece's finest made life uncomfortable for us in Athens but didn't really look anything to be scared of. Especially in this warm climate, away from the wintry weather of Athens. Joe Cole hits the post after two minutes, but it takes just four minutes more for us to go in front, with Ballack heading in a Lampard cross, and it's just what we need to settle us down. From then on, we never look in trouble. Frank makes it 2-0 and in the second half Kalou gets a third. Job done, and done very well. Carlo plays in goal because Cech's picked up another injury but he has virtually nothing to do.

Into the last 16 and to be honest it was very easy. Tougher tasks probably await – we could be up against Man United, Arsenal or Barcelona next. But if we could get Schalke, Fenerbahce or even Liverpool in the next round, I'd be very hopeful of making yet another semi-final.

I wonder if any Olympiacos fans got conned into paying £25 for a beer and a glass of grape juice in a taverna off Oxford Street? If they did, they'd better be careful if they walk round Trafalgar Square tomorrow.

Saturday March 8
Barnsley (away)

When the FA Cup quarter-final draw gave us a trip to Oakwell I was sorely tempted to head north but already had other plans.

After much umming and ahhing, I decide to settle for watching the game on TV.

Earlier in the day Man United surprisingly lost 1-0 at home to Portsmouth. It's a big shock and great for us – we're red-hot favourites to win the trophy now.

A friend of mine from work, Sarah, is from Barnsley. She's at the match and texts me to say how excited she is. It's a huge game for them and unlike when they knocked out Liverpool in the last round, they're at home this time, so there'll be more Barnsley fans there.

The fact they knocked out Liverpool shows they are not to be under-estimated. Having said that, the last time we went to Oakwell we won 6-0, with Vialli hitting four. But the last time we played Barnsley in the FA Cup we lost 4-0 – 19 years ago but I remember it all too well.

We start poorly. We've left out too many first-choice players for my liking. Lampard (who isn't suspended – his sending-off against the Hammers was overturned), Drogba, Makelele and Ashley Cole are nowhere in sight and Kalou only on the bench. Has Grant learnt nothing from what Barnsley did to a weakened Liverpool?

Barnsley have a big hulking striker up front, Kayode Odejayi, who makes life difficult for Terry and Carvalho but thankfully doesn't seem to know how to shoot. He hasn't scored a goal since September – 28 games. That's the sort of record that makes Robert Fleck and Chris Sutton look prolific.

Odejayi spurns a couple of decent chances in the first half and we get to the break at 0-0, having played poorly. Anelka and Malouda look completely unsuited to this sort of match while Wright-Phillips is anonymous and the defence shaky. At half-time I think we can't possibly play that badly again in the second half, but we do. With 25 minutes left Wayne Bridge goes with a runner instead of blocking the man with the ball and the great cross sent over as a result sees Odejayi – Mr No-goals-since-the-clocks-went-back – climb above Cudicini and head into the net.

It's a fully deserved lead. And thanks to half our star players being given the day off we don't even have many options to turn it around. Kalou and Pizarro come on, but Pizarro has only scored two all season and is another man not used to trips to take on battling Championship teams from the South Yorkshire economic deprivation area. We chuck everything at Barnsley in a frantic finish but it finishes 1-0.

Barnsley's fans go wild, flooding on to the pitch. I don't begrudge them a second of it, their players were better and wanted it more. We were awful. Joe Cole was the best player on show, but our others were probably the 10 worst.

Avram Grant led us to a Carling Cup final defeat via bewildering tactics, now he's rested several of our best players and taken us to our first FA Cup exit against a lower division team since 1995. It isn't good enough. Sarah texts me after the final whistle asking, "How did that happen?" I'd like to know too. I reply saying well done and it was fully deserved. Because it was.

Monday March 10

Barnsley are drawn against Cardiff in the semi-finals. So all that stood between us and the cup final was Barnsley and Cardiff – two teams in the bottom half of the Championship.

On Facebook, the group "Avram Grant Out!! Out!! Out!!" has 43 more members, "You can stick Avram Grant up your arse" has 38 more, "I could be a better manager for Chelsea than Avram Grant" has 25 newcomers and "Avram Grant – you've won me over!!" has seen two people leave. "Petition to get Avram Grant sacked from CFC and blown to the moon" has three more members.

Wednesday March 12
Derby County (home)

We need some cheering up. And what better way than by taking on Derby, probably the worst side ever to play in the

Premier League? They've won one of their 29 games and have just 10 points.

We nearly score with our first attack when Lampard hits the post but Derby put the whole team behind the ball and look like they'd give anything for a 0-0 draw. It takes almost half an hour for the deadlock to be broken, with Lamps scoring on 28 minutes. Kalou adds a second before the break and the game is won by half-time.

By far the highlight of the first half is Dan revealing he owns a Dalek, which sits next to his bed at home. Dan is immensely proud of his Dalek – it's life-size and was far from cheap – but the news that our friend, who is in his late twenties, sleeps next to Dr Who's mortal enemy amuses Mark and I so much we can hardly concentrate on the match. Mark wants to know what women think when Dan takes them back only to find they'll be sharing a room with a Dalek. Tim starts shouting "Exterminate!" at Dan and a bloke in the row in front wants to know if he goes to away games in a Tardis. At one point I have tears in my eyes, I'm laughing so much. Dan will never, ever forget today.

The second half starts and Derby remain Sylvester McCoy to our Tom Baker. We plough through them with all the efficiency and ruthlessness of the Cybermen and score four goals in a 15 minute spell. Lampard makes it 3-0, Joe adds the fourth and then Frank gets two more. He's the first midfielder to score four goals in a Premier League match. I know we're only playing Derby but what a player.

My friend Ralfe is an Ipswich fan and for years has been weighed down by the stigma of his team holding the record for the worst defeat since the Premiership began – 9-0 at Old Trafford in 1995. We're six up with 18 minutes left and I text him to say the record could be under threat. Just as I'm sending it there's a small murmur from the Derby fans in the Shed End. I look up and see they've scored. The game peters out and we win 6-1. Obviously it's great to win 6-1, but it's tempered by two things; Derby are truly awful and we still have the Barnsley and Tottenham results hanging over us. Tonight's been great but it's still not right.

As I stroll along Fulham Road I phone dad to give him a match report. While I walk and talk I notice people are shouting and staring up at a window in one of the houses on the left. I glance up and see two very attractive young women standing in the window in their underwear. Needless to say I continue to gaze up there and walk straight into a bloke standing innocently on the pavement. He goes flying, I nearly go over and I just about manage to hold on to my phone, even if I haven't held on to my dignity. We've won 6-1, Spurs have gone out of the Uefa Cup on penalties and my life's turning into a scene from a Carry On film. I call that a good night.

Weighed down by Dalek-inspired guilt, I text Dan and tell him so that he can laugh at me too.

Saturday March 14
Sunderland (away)

My mate John, an old friend from school I shared a flat with for years, is up for the weekend with his fiancée Katherine. Katherine is originally from Leicestershire and a Leicester City fan. And as Leicester are away to West Brom the three of us go to the game. I keep a close eye on events at the Stadium of Light, checking the score on my phone every few minutes. I soon discover Terry has put us 1-0 up after 10 minutes. It's his first goal for us in 19 months and turns out to be the only goal of the game.

At the Hawthorns we're surrounded by Leicester fans who've seen their team fall deep into relegation trouble. West Brom, by contrast, are pushing for promotion. The mood is one of apprehension and it gets worse when the home side go 1-0 up. But then West Brom have a player sent off and the game turns. By the end, struggling Leicester have won 4-1.

Katherine is absolutely overjoyed. The Leicester fans can hardly contain their delight – or their surprise. They're ecstatic and it's a wonderful atmosphere to be in.

As we head back to my flat Katherine is skipping down the road singing "4-1, 4-1". It strikes me then why I've enjoyed today so much. It's been wonderful supporting Chelsea over the past few trophy-laden years and I really wouldn't change a thing (apart from the manager...). But because we expect to win virtually every game I'd forgotten how brilliant it is to see your team get a result against the odds. It's the first time in ages I've experienced the unique joy of a completely unexpected win, and it's not even my team who've managed it.

Wednesday March 19
Tottenham (away)

For the second time in five days Chelsea have an important away match and I'm at a completely different stadium watching a completely different game.

But unlike Saturday I'm arguably even more devoted to the Chelsea cause than those who made their way to Three Point Lane. I'm at my first ever youth team game, watching our young 'uns trying to reach the FA Youth Cup final for the first time in 47 years. The second leg of their semi-final at Villa Park is nicely poised after a 1-1 draw in the home leg. Villa are letting everyone in for free and have advertised the game quite well, so I'm among a crowd of nearly 11,000 and I appear to be one of about three Chelsea fans. I take a seat in the Holte End and soon realise I'm surrounded by thousands of easily-distracted children, who squeal a lot and make paper planes out of their programmes. I feel very old.

Villa go a goal up after three minutes but after that we take control and play some very nice football. We equalise through a cracking shot from Sergio Tejera and take the lead with a great run and finish from Gael Kakuta. The start of the second half coincides with kick-off at Spurs so I spend the remainder of the game watching the action in front of me while paying more attention to the radio commentary of the first team. Villa equalise but we clinch a 3-2 win through Adam Philip and are into the final for the first time since 1961. Chelsea's youngsters fully deserve the win and look really good – the future is bright..

But what of the present? Drogba puts us one up after just three minutes, Woodgate equalises, probably with the side of his face again, and with less than 20 minutes gone we're back in front thanks to Essien. The second half brings more goals as I make my way home from Villa Park, still listening to the radio and fending off chit-chat from Villa fans who think I'm one of them. I'm walking to Aston station as Joe Cole puts us 3-1 up, surely clinching the win. But as I stand on the platform Berbatov pulls one back and when I'm on the train Huddlestone equalises. I'm walking through New Street station as Joe puts us back in front and surely that's it? No – as I walk back to my flat Robbie Keane equalises on 88 minutes. And as I get into the lift Carlo makes an apparently stunning save from Berbatov to stop us losing a game we should have won.

I watch the highlights and it's a cracker. But I'd have taken a dull 1-0 win any time. And, at the risk of reprising an old theme, you can't help thinking we would have got one under Jose. This is our second 4-4 draw of the season, both involving conceding late equalisers. We're only five points behind Man United. What a difference two wins could have made.

Sunday March 23
Arsenal (home)

It's Easter Sunday and the weekend you hope will bring love-ly spring weather, conjuring up images of baby rabbits frolick-ing in a field in bright sunshine, has seen most of the country covered in snow. It's absolutely freezing. I arrive in London in time to watch Manchester United v Liverpool in the pub. Could the Scousers do us a favour and take something from the game? Of course not. United win 3-0.

We're unbeaten at home in the league since we lost to Arsenal four years ago near the end of Claudio Ranieri's reign. Months ago I earmarked today's game as the one which would see the record go but in recent weeks Arsenal have gone to pieces. They lost 5-1 to Spurs in the Carling Cup, 4-0 to Man United in the FA Cup and have drawn their last four league games – the highlight a 2-2 draw with Birmingham which saw Gallas go nuts, kicking advertising hoardings and bursting into tears. As a result I now don't expect us to lose.

Arsenal are typical Arsenal with nice passing football and no end product. They come close a few times in the first half but Carlo makes a couple of good saves and Gallas – who gets a predictably rough reception on his first return to the Bridge – heads against a post. We also have chances but can't take any of them. It's fairly even.

Just before the hour Sagna meets a corner with a glancing header and because we've got nobody on the post the ball sneaks in to the net. We're making too many basic defensive errors lately. We show no real signs of pulling level and 10 minutes later Grant makes changes. Anelka and Belletti are on and we move to 4-4-2. But the removal of Ballack is unpopular with the fans, prompting deafening choruses of "You don't know what you're doing!", with the odd "Jose Mourinho!" chucked in for good measure.

But within two minutes Drogba equalises and, with eight minutes left, Anelka heads a Joe Cole cross on to Drogba and it's 2-1. What a turnaround, Drogba moves yet closer to all-time-great status and we're all forced to admit that maybe Grant did know what he was doing after all. Though, having said that, we'd gone behind and he threw on an extra striker. I reckon I could have worked that out.

But this is not the time to be churlish. It looked like we were going to lose and we haven't. We've shown real grit to come from behind to win. We've extended our unbeaten home run. We've beaten old foes who are one of our two big rivals for the title. And we've gone second in the league – above them. It's a day for celebration.

As I bounce along King's Road back to Victoria coach station I notice everyone is smiling. But when I reach Sloane Square it starts to snow again. Climate change evidently doesn't check the football scores.

Sunday March 30
Middlesbrough (home)

If we're going to challenge United at the top of the table we need to win games like this. And we get off to a great start, Ricky Carvalho heading us in front from a Wayne Bridge free-kick on six minutes.

Will this good start lead to a comfortable victory? Sadly, no. Drogba, Ballack and Terry all come close but it stays 1-0. Shaun Wright-Phillips comes on and makes the sort of impact which explains why I think he's an absolute waste of space who shouldn't be anywhere near our team. He has two chances within a couple of minutes. The first he pulls wide and the second, with only the keeper to beat from the edge of the area, he skies so badly I fear the ball may go over the stand and land somewhere near Ealing.

He drives me mad and I hope we get rid of him this summer. The good form he showed in January has completely evaporated and he's back to snatching at shots, playing passes to people who aren't there, running into cul-de-sacs and crossing like a poor man's Jesper Gronkjaer.

We're almost punished for his profligacy when Carlo races out of his net to cut out a long pass, only to completely miss the ball. Alves is faced with guiding the ball into an empty net but manages to smack it against the post.

In the last 10 minutes an amazing goalmouth melee from a corner sees Alves and Wheater both head against our bar before a third Boro player blasts it over. We hold on for a scrappy 1-0 win. They say the ability to grind out wins when you're not playing well is the sign of a good team. What about the ability to shamble your way to a 1-0 win against a team from the bottom half who would have won if the woodwork hadn't come to your rescue? What's that a sign of?

Chapter 9

Drama, glory and Thursday nights

Wednesday April 2
Fenerbahce (away)

After Trondheim and Athens it's time to save some money so this is one for TV viewing.

Last time we played in Turkey we won 5-0 away to Galatasaray on my 24th birthday in our Champions League run under Gianluca Vialli. I'm not expecting the same tonight, but I'm quietly confident. When you get to the last eight of the Champions League you expect the likes of Barcelona or Milan so to get Fenerbahce is hardly a bad draw.

We take the lead through an own goal from Brazilian Deivid (which appears to be Brazilian for David) and everything seems to be going to plan. We dominate the rest of the first half, Essien hits the bar, Drogba has two decent chances and Lampard also comes close.

In the second half we continue to stroll without hitting a second and Fenerbahce bring on Colin Kazim-Richards, formerly of Bury, Brighton and Sheffield United. Within five minutes he's beaten the offside trap, outpaced Carvalho and hammered the ball past Cudicini. He only scored once all last season when Sheffield United got relegated and has only got one previous goal for the Turks this season, in a 10-3 win (seriously) against lower division opposition in a cup. But he can score against us.

Suddenly we can hardly get out of our half and it's all Fenerbahce. With 10 minutes left own-goal man Deivid gets the ball 35 yards out, looks up, sees he has nobody to pass to and does the only thing he can. Hammer the ball right into the top left corner of the net. We were so dominant and now we're losing. We spend the rest of the game trying not to let in a third.

It's a ridiculous result given how much we bossed the first hour, but a 1-0 win at home would put us through, so it's not the end of the world.

Grant claims it's a good result, a very honest and eloquent Michael Ballack admits "It's our fault" and all the pundits on Sky – Gus Poyet, Ray Parlour, Phil Thompson, Gordon Strachan and Graeme Souness – say we'll definitely go through. Souness says we'll win the competition. Hmmm.

Saturday April 5
Manchester City (away)

I'm at work today so I'm following the game at Eastlands remotely but news comes through that we've gone in front through a Richard Dunne own goal. Of course we beat them 6-0 at home but I'd still settle for 1-0 this time. So when Kalou makes it 2-0 in the second half, I'm very content.

It's also Grand National Day. There's a horse running called Chelsea Harbour and I feel obliged to stick some money on it, on the basis that if a horse with Chelsea in its name romped home in the National and I hadn't backed it, I'd feel pretty cheesed off. Our equine namesake runs a good race, handily placed for most of it and leading for quite a while. And when he does fade the one I got in our work sweepstake storms to the front and stays there. Fifty quid and three points. Not a bad day at all.

Tuesday April 8
Fenerbahce (home)

It's another free flag day at the Bridge, but I've got so many now I don't bother picking one up. There's a bloke with two sons on my left and I let them have all the flags in our vicinity. I'm nice like that.

The reason they're sat there is that yet again hardly any of the usual faces are here. I can understand John and Margaret not coming up from Cornwall for a game that would cost them £90 for the tickets, plus petrol money, and probably see them get home at about 4am when it's on television anyway. But I'm surprised at how many of the London-based regulars aren't around. It's a Champions League quarter-final after all. The only faces I recognise are the same two blokes in the row in front, who again acknowledge me as the only other "loyal fan" around. Even Big Sam's missing, which must be a first.

You can tell people haven't been here often before when they sing, "When the Blues go marching in" instead of "steaming in". The bloke on my right sings that and keeps slagging off Drogba, which suggests to me that he wasn't here for the Arsenal game, missed the whole of last season, didn't see last year's FA Cup final or any of the three League Cup finals he's scored in. He's also forgotten the only goal against Barcelona last season, the 15 other Champions League goals he's scored for us and the 35-yard last minute winner at Everton last year. I could go on...

Of course we're a goal behind coming into the game, but only until the fourth minute when a Lampard free-kick from the wing is headed in by Ballack. One of the blokes in front turns to me and says "It's a bit too long to hold on isn't it?" But that's more or less what we try to do. Joe Cole hits the post but otherwise we sit back a bit too much for my liking. It's reminiscent of last week – we're clearly the better side but don't kill it off and Fenerbahce are a threat.

Matters aren't helped by Carlo getting a hamstring injury midway through the first half. On comes Hilario – it's amazing how many times in the past five years we've had our third choice keeper playing in vital games. Hilario played a large chunk of last season and in Ranieri's last year we had Marco Ambrosio playing in a Champions League semi. We get to half time 1-0 up and going through as things stand, but if they score once we're out.

Early in the second half it arrives, tonight's Mystifying Grant

Substitution, as right-back Belletti comes on for left winger Kalou. I have no idea what formation we're supposed to be playing now, and for 10 minutes the players haven't either. Fenerbahce come in to the game more and more, Hilario makes a couple of fantastic saves to keep us in front and "We're supposed to be at home" rings round the ground, reflecting the fact the visitors have been allowed to take the game to us. It's tonight's version of "You don't know what you're doing".

But with three minutes to go Essien gets round the left back and threads the ball through to Lampard, who taps in from right in front of goal. We're through.

At Anfield Liverpool have beaten Arsenal 4-2 in what sounds like a fantastic game, so for the third time in four seasons we'll play the Scousers in the semis. Surely, surely, we can't lose a third time? If we get through it means Grant will have done what Jose couldn't, and I'm not sure I want that, but then again of course I want us to beat Liverpool and win the Champions League. The club comes first but these are confusing times.

I did a 10-hour shift at work before heading down to the match and get home just after 2am having been up since 5am. Am I loyal, or stupid? Probably both.

Monday April 14
Wigan (home)

Wigan on a Monday night. Oh, the glamour of supporting a big team in the Premier League.

Roadworks on the M1 delay my coach for more than an hour, with the journey taking four hours instead of two hours 50 minutes. Thankfully I set off early and the delay doesn't stop me getting there for kick-off. Mark arrives brandishing his medal from the previous day's London Marathon. It took him a bit more than four hours and I find myself thinking "He nearly ran a marathon in the time I spent on that coach", but I'm not sure what conclusions I come to. The coach did travel more than 26 miles, after all. He admits he was overtaken by a Womble but doesn't know which one it was, much to Tim's disappointment. Let's hope it wasn't Madame Cholet.

No doubt influenced by the fact we've got another game in three days, Grant leaves out Drogba and Carvalho, while Joe Cole is only on the bench. And the team is weakened further still when Frank pulls out for personal reasons shortly before kick-off. Apparently his mum is ill.

It's fairly mundane stuff and you'd never know we're in with a good chance of winning the league. Around me everyone is a bit distracted, not least Big Sam who at one point keeps himself busy by miming counting the tiny handful of Wigan fans. One hand over the straining eyes, the other pointing and counting. Textbook Big Sam.

Malouda is an absolute waste of space yet again and when Cole comes on for him at half-time things improve immediately. Terry volleys against the bar from a corner, Kirkland makes another fantastic save from Kalou but then – within a minute of those two chances – Michael Essien finally puts us in front with a good finish from 20 yards.

From here on we should kill the game off but we can't get a second goal. That's arguably no problem while we're winning, but in injury time Emile Heskey scores an equaliser. The funny thing is, when the goal goes in we don't cry, we don't scream, we don't stand around staring silently into the distance in disbelief. After a brief swear I think the first thing I say is "Oh well, that's that then..." Mark, Dan, John and I chat for a while and agree we haven't been the best team in the country this season and sadly the Mancs have. It wouldn't have been fair if we'd finished above them and at least now we can stop this "If United drop points here and we win there, we'd only need to beat them and then hope that they draw with xyz for us to win the league..." nonsense.

Don't get me wrong. I wanted to win the league, of course I did. But in those two years we were champions under Jose we were head and shoulders above everyone else. We simply aren't anymore and we've got what we deserve. I think back to what Chris said after the win at Birmingham in January: "If we win the Premier League, the rest of the Premier League should hang their heads in shame." I just didn't expect it to be finished off with an incredibly average ineptitude-riddled slip-up at home to Wigan.

Thursday April 17
Everton (away)

I should have been at this game, but I'm not, thanks to Rupert Murdoch.

The match was supposed to be this Saturday but less than three weeks ago, after tickets went on sale, it got moved to Thursday night because Sky wanted to televise it. Both clubs were fuming and apparently tried to get it changed back, but the Premier League weren't interested in helping fans get to a game. I'd arranged to meet up before the game with my old friend Neil, an Everton fan, but now neither of us can go. I'm working until 10pm, which obviously rules me out, and my attempts at swapping shifts failed.

On top of the inconvenience for fans, there's also the issue of us having our two consecutive 'weekend' games on Monday and Thursday – just three days apart – while Manchester United get a six-day gap. Hardly fair, but there's plenty that's unfair in modern football and we've benefited from some of it.

Chelsea do come out of this with some credit. After failing to get the match moved to a more sensible time, the club has used the Sky money to pay for the fans' tickets for the game and to lay on free coach and train travel from London to Liverpool and back. This has got a brief mention in the press, but only a brief one. Wouldn't want to be seen saying good things about Chelsea would they?

So I get a refund on the £28 I've paid for my ticket but I didn't want a refund – I wanted to go to the game. Instead I hand my ticket to Dan so he can take a mate with him. As I'm working I don't even get to see it on Sky. I manage to listen to most of it on the radio and, with Lampard still missing, we get an excellent 1-0 win thanks to a second of the week from Michael 'goal machine' Essien.

We're two points behind Man United, but they've got a game in hand. While the world waits for Thursday night football to take off, I can't see us finishing anything but second. And I'm still fuming over the match being moved.

Tuesday April 22
Liverpool (away)

For the second time in five days I narrowly avoid going to Merseyside. Had the game been tomorrow I would probably have gone, but today's my mum's birthday, I'm off work and I've been at my parents' place in Sussex for a long weekend. So while my preparation for the game could have been a train into Lime Street and then the journey out to Stanley Park, keeping any sign of a London accent under wraps, instead I have a very nice day out in Eastbourne, including a journey along the seafront on the Dotto Train, a trip to the pier to win some cuddly toys for my nephew Toby and a slice of lemon meringue pie in a cafe. Unquestionably the right choice.

The added bonus is I can watch the game with my parents. The last time I watched a match with them was when we lost to Barnsley, so let's hope that's not a portent of bad tidings. It wouldn't be good for Chez Parents to establish itself as an unlucky venue. Of course this is the third time in four years we've played the Scousers in a Champions League semi-final, and the only year we didn't we played them in the group stages. You get to meet any team from anywhere in Europe and you end up with a trip to Anfield four years running. The law of averages dictates we must surely win this time and I go into the game fairly confident. But Liverpool always raise their game for Europe and have knocked out Inter and Arsenal already.

Inevitably ITV make a big deal of You'll Never Walk Alone and go on and on about the special atmosphere. I prefer to think about the fact that we're better than Liverpool. The last time they finished above us was six years ago.

The match is a bit of a battle, predictably tense. Liverpool get more chances in the first half, but they are the home side. It looks like we're reaching half-time at 0-0 until two minutes before the break we get caught out from a quick free-kick and Kuyt makes it 1-0. The goal spoils the mood in the Clarke household, but we aren't too despondent. These semi-finals against Liverpool have never been easy and it's not the first setback we've had.

The second half starts with Liverpool on the front foot, boosted by the goal. Babel comes close to a second and we are hanging on. Drogba is being kicked all over the place by the Liverpool defence, but that's partly because he's giving them a torrid time. He's playing well but is too isolated.

As we go into five minutes of injury time dad and I discuss how 1-0 isn't the end of the world. We were 1-0 up at this stage last year and ended up going out, so there's no reason why we can't turn it around too. And then, in the 95th minute, Kalou gets the ball down by the corner flag, does really well to get round a couple of defenders and sends over a cracking cross. Anelka and Drogba are in the box but it's a red shirt that gets there first. Instead of scooping it over the bar or hooking it away with his right foot, John Arne Riise instead elects for a diving header. Straight past Reina and into the back of the net.

Dad and I leap out of our seats. Mum can't believe that having watched nearly all of the game she'd wandered into the hall when the goal went in. It's such a let-off. I'd certainly settled for 1-0 and was secretly quite grateful we weren't further behind. But that equaliser makes such a difference.

I get inundated with texts from friends within seconds. Mark says "What a great Liverpool substitution! John Arne Rescue!" Dan goes for "Yeah Ginger Twat!" But it's not just Chelsea fans who are pleased. I hear from delighted Everton, Ipswich and

Oldham fans and an old mate from university, Danny, who supports Tottenham, says: "Ha ha that is so funny!" If even Spurs fans are glad, Liverpool must be very unpopular.

Saturday April 26
Manchester United (home)

This is our first home league game on a Saturday since we played Spurs 15 weeks ago, which shows how much football has changed over the years. And of course this one is not at 3pm. As a potential title decider it's on TV so it's a lunchtime kick-off.

This means an early start when you have to travel down from Birmingham and I'm on the 8am coach. I've had a few late nights this week so having to get up that early was a bit of an effort. I drift off to sleep within a couple of minutes of leaving Birmingham coach station and the next thing I know the driver's voice is coming from the speakers saying "Ladies and gentlemen, we are now arriving at London Victoria coach station".

I've slept the entire way, more than two-and-a-half hours, and get out of the coach in a drowsy stupor. And I don't have the option of staying in bed for a few minutes or putting on my dressing gown and vegetating in front of the TV with a bowl of cereal. Instead I'm propelled on to the posh streets of Belgravia, wandering past the £4 million houses while thinking "But I've only just woken up..."

It's an absolutely beautiful day. We've bypassed spring and gone straight from winter to summer. The sun is shining, it's lovely and warm. As I walk through Sloane Square and on to King's Road my mind goes back to five weeks ago when I got snowed on in this very spot. Today I'm more in danger of getting sunstroke.

Frank Lampard's not playing. His mother died on Thursday, aged 58. That's five years younger than my mum and no age at all. We sing his name before kick-off and there's a minute's applause in her memory, which ends with more singing of his name. I'm sure we'd show respect for the parents of any player, but Frank is massively popular among Chelsea fans and he's often said how close he was to his mum, so it seems all the more important to make sure the tributes are right.

In the first half we're all over United, playing lovely football and having all the possession. Joe Cole hits the bar, we have a decent shout for a penalty, we're bossing midfield and when United attack our defence is in control. Just before half-time we get our reward. Drogba sends over a great cross from the right and Ballack heads past van der Sar. It's fully deserved – it's been very one-sided and we've played our best half of football of the season.

We look just as comfortable in the second half until 11 minutes in when Ricky Carvalho, excellent so far, plays the ball without looking straight to the feet of Wayne Rooney. The bulldog-getting-it's-arse-slapped-while-chewing-a-wasp-faced one sprints away with the ball and slots it into the net, his first-ever goal against us. It's really not deserved, we've been so on top.

Rooney goes off almost straight away, replaced by Ronaldo. Ashley Cole has the prancer in his pocket and he never looks likely to inflict any damage on us, except for a couple of free-kicks which go straight into the wall. This half is more even, but we're still playing very well and push for a winner. Anelka and Shevchenko come on and we're playing something like a 3-3-4 formation. We have a clear penalty denied when Wes Brown handles the ball. I could see it from row BB, but the ref couldn't. A couple of minutes later Carrick blocks an Essien cross with an outstretched arm and the linesman does signal for a penalty. The stadium erupts. And it hasn't even gone in yet.

Ballack grabs the ball and van der Sar and Silvestre do their best to put him off – Silvestre being particularly childish, picking up blades of grass and throwing them in Ballack's face. It's the behaviour of a 10-year-old and a naughty one at that. But if there's one nationality you can't put off when it comes to penalties, it's the Germans. Ballack hammers his penalty into the back of the net. Stamford Bridge goes mad. Dan tries to pick me up and soon regrets it when he remembers I'm hardly waif-like. Margaret can hardly watch. The match that is, not me being lifted three inches off the ground.

There's still time for more drama, with Ashley Cole and Sheva both clearing goal-bound efforts off the line, but after five minutes of injury time the whistle goes. We celebrate like we've just won the league and the players do similar. We sing along to Blue is the Colour and Kalinka and dance to One Step Beyond. Margaret is in tears. The atmosphere today has been fantastic, the best I can remember for at least a couple of years, maybe longer. Singing for 90 minutes, deafening support, the sun shining on us as we react to the importance of the game and the quality of the performance. It's how it should be and I hope it's the same against Liverpool on Wednesday.

I don't know what to think about this season anymore. Less than a fortnight ago I accepted it was over. For most of the past seven months I've wanted the manager out. But what now? We could win the league and Champions League. Maybe Grant's done a great job? Or are the players carrying themselves along, winning games and challenging for the big prizes despite the manager rather than because of him? I really don't know. But I do know it's the players I feel proud of today. They were all superb, especially two-goal Ballack, who has been our best player in the second half of the season.

I go off to meet some old friends from university for a few drinks in Covent Garden. I've got the Chelsea shirt on, of course, and on the bus and Tube loads of people smile at me or give me a thumbs up. It's been a great day to be a Chelsea fan. I've been lucky enough to have some really happy days at Stamford Bridge. This was one of the happiest.

Wednesday 30 April
Liverpool (home)

And on to the next instalment. It's the fourth time I've seen us play in a Champions League semi-final, but the first time I've headed for the second leg feeling hopeful. In 2004 we were already 3-1 down to Monaco from the first leg and I expected us to go out, then when we played Liverpool in 2005 and 2007 I went to the first legs at home and watched us agonisingly eliminated in the returns on TV. But this time we just need a win, or even a 0-0 draw, at home to a team who aren't as good as us. And on top of that, we can't lose to Liverpool in the semis for the third time in four years, surely?

As I wait for the coach a bloke spots the badge on my Chelsea fleece and asks if I've got any spares. It's the first time I've ever been asked 100 miles from the stadium, six hours before kickoff. When I tell him I haven't, he heads off to ask a bloke in a Liverpool shirt. He could have a long day. The coach driver announces it's the service to London Victoria, unless it gets too late and we'll have to be dropped off at Stamford Bridge, because that's where he's going this evening. Good lad.

I arrive in London to find pouring rain, in marked contrast to Saturday, and it doesn't stop until after the game's finished. The weather means I catch the Tube from Sloane Square and the songs of praise for Fernando Torres from some Scousers in my carriage remind me of one of the main reasons I've taken to walking to the ground.

I head up the lucky left-hand flight of stairs at Fulham Broadway and towards the ground. Everyone is soaked but the mood seems good. Unlike the previous European games, nearly all the usual faces are here. The only absentee is Dan, who realised too late that tickets had gone on sale. He should have asked his mate the Time Lord to pop back for one.

Again there are flags for everyone and just like Saturday we're in good voice. I'm so pleased we are – I've grown heartily sick of hearing Liverpool fans, players and ex-players say over the past week that Stamford Bridge isn't an intimidating place. The fact we haven't lost here for four years suggests otherwise. True, it goes quiet too often these days. Tonight it doesn't. As close to 40,000 voices sing along with Blue Is The Colour, led by a

Chelsea-supporting opera singer on the pitch, I wonder if they're showing this on TV, in the way they ALWAYS show the Scousers singing You'll Never Walk Alone? I think we can safely bet they aren't.

Frank's back in the team, just six days after his mother's death. It's a brave decision, for him and for Avram Grant, but I'm sure neither of them would have made it if they weren't sure. He'll want to win for his mum. Drogba is another who'll be keen to do well tonight, because that twat Benitez has spent all week slagging him off for diving. I'd love to see him ram the words down that goateed throat. I'm not going to pretend Didier doesn't fall over a bit, but he's hardly alone. Has Benitez never seen Steven Gerrard play, for example?

We start well, with Drogba lively and Salomon Kalou having a cracking game. On 33 minutes Frank puts Kalou away, Reina pushes his shot into the path of the advancing Drogba and he smashes the rebound in. 1-0! The crowd goes berserk. As we all leap around I'm prevented from totally losing my inhibitions by the fact my glasses have nearly flown off my face. I just about hold them on. I couldn't have them fall off and be stamped on, I want to be able to see the rest of the game.

The flags are back out for a while and the Scousers are silent. We've been well on top and go in one-up at half-time, having played very well. It's the least we deserve. We discuss the cost of getting to Moscow for the final. It's not complacency – it's due to the fact the programme reveals the official trips are £749 plus the price of the ticket and the visa, and the day that should go by uncommented on is still some way off. The general mood is one of "I can't afford that".

Liverpool improve in the second half and 20 minutes in Benayoun waltzes through our defence and plays in Torres, who has slipped his marker. 1-1. Now it's Liverpool's turn to make some noise and on the pitch they look more likely to score. When it goes to extra time I'm thinking "Surely not again?" and fearing penalties. Margaret says "We're going to lose" and I reply with a far-from-certain "No we're not".

Extra time starts, and we're on top again. We begin to make chances, and suddenly Essien follows up after a shot is blocked and hammers the ball home from outside the area. We're back in front and we all go berserk again. It must be 30 seconds before we realise the ref has disallowed it. No idea what for. Was that our chance? Has it gone?

A minute later Hyypia brings down Ballack and the ref points to the spot. What a chance. Of course Lampard is our penalty taker but after the events of the past week – on and off the pitch – I hope Ballack takes it. But he doesn't. Frank has the ball. He's doing this for his mum and if he misses it will be terrible.

He doesn't!

As everyone leaps around for the second time in a couple of minutes I find I can't. My legs won't lift me off the ground. That was a hugely emotional moment in a hugely important game and I have a lump in my throat. It doesn't stop me cheering and shouting, but I do feel completely drained. Frank looks in tears and celebrates with the rest of the team before pointing up to the sky and then to his dad in the stand. What a moment.

We're back in front and back on top and a few minutes later it's 3-1. Anelka makes a great run and picks out Didier who smashes home another. Thanks for firing him up Rafa. We're there now, surely? Well, there's one last scare – Ryan Babel shoots from about 40 yards and Petr Cech can only palm it in to the top corner. Some Liverpool fans have already gone. Three minutes left and if they score again, we're out. But they don't. We hold on and we're through.

If the scenes after the game on Saturday were amazing, what's tonight like? We're all singing, waving the flags, hugging each other, clambering over seats to hug those who are too far away to reach and cheering the players, who are celebrating with similar passion on the pitch.

The songs are all played – Kalinka, Blue Is The Colour, The Liquidator, One Step Beyond, and the one that goes "der-der-da-

der der-der-da-der" and has a line about "you have to laugh or
else you'd cry".

After what seems like ages we begin to go our separate ways.
Talk turns again to the cost of getting to the final. A few of us
have serious doubts about going, including me, but I can't
believe Chelsea can get to the Champions League final without
me there. On the other hand, even if we win could it possibly
beat tonight for excitement, emotion and joy?

I booked myself on the midnight coach in case it went to extra
time and it's a good job I did. But it leaves me more than an hour
to get to Victoria. I walk as far as Earls Court with Mark then
pop into a pub for a quick pint and carry on celebrating with a
random Scottish stranger who'd watched it in there. It's great
being a football fan. It's great being a Chelsea fan. And this has
been a great week to be a Chelsea fan.

I get home about 3am and watch the goals again on Sky. I don't
want the night to end.

Chapter 10

Right to the end

Thursday May 1

An amazing April ended with me wondering how I could afford to get to Moscow. And May begins with me concluding I can't. I'm not going to the Champions League final.

I spend hours today on the internet, looking for flights to Moscow via Germany, via Switzerland, via Austria, via Italy, via Latvia. Most of them are going for extortionate prices. It doesn't help that Man United fans had a 24-hour head start and snapped up what few bargains there may have been.

There are trains and coaches, which are a lot cheaper but bring problems of their own. Getting either a train or coach directly across Europe involves going through Belarus, which means getting two visas for there, one for the outward journey and one for the way back, as well as the visa for Russia. I don't fancy my chances of sorting that out in less than three weeks.

I find flights from Bristol to Riga, the capital of Latvia, for £49 return. And you can get a train from Riga to Moscow for about £100, so on paper this looks promising. But I would have to fly out on the Sunday – three days before the match – and there are no hotel rooms available anywhere in Moscow. I don't much fancy sleeping on those streets.

Of course I could travel with the club, which is how I'd planned to do it from the moment it looked like we might reach the final. But while I'd thought the day trip might cost about £500, maybe £600 all in, it's £749 just to fly out there, plus at least £67 for the match ticket, more for the visa and of course whatever you spend on the day. It'll be at least a grand. I think about biting the bullet and booking it until I hear on the radio the Russian authorities are so scared of trouble they aren't going to let any day-trip fans free in the city. You'd arrive at the airport, get taken straight to the stadium and then after the match be escorted straight back to the airport.

It would be ludicrous enough going to Moscow for the day, but to pay £1,000 or more to go to Moscow for the day and not even see Red Square, the Kremlin or St Basil's Cathedral? You must be joking. My season ticket is only £650 and people say that's expensive. How can I justify spending one-and-a-half times that on one match? I'm not going to go. A thousand pounds for a football match? You have to draw the line somewhere and, like Hitler, my line is this side of Moscow.

I'm certainly not alone. During the day I hear from both Mark and Tim who are not going. We've all supported Chelsea for years, all had season tickets for years (those two both longer than me) and we all go to loads of games. Last night was my 33rd game of this season – 34th if you include the youth team match. I've earned the right to see my club play in what's probably the biggest match in its history and I've been robbed by Uefa deciding to hold the Champions League final in such an impractical place.

I'm not saying finals should only ever be in Western Europe. I'm not saying all decisions should be taken to suit the requirements of English fans. But they shouldn't be holding a final in a city you need a visa to get into and which has nowhere near enough hotel rooms.

Admittedly, I could get there. Whenever there's a high-profile match in a tricky place to reach you hear tales of people getting there by trains, planes and automobiles. But it looks like I'd be doing it on my own, and I don't much fancy travelling the width of Europe alone. I can just see myself missing a connecting train in Riga or losing my passport in Minsk.

The more I think about it, the more I reckon I've made the

right decision. But I feel robbed of my right to be there. I'm no part-timer, I've already been to Greece and Norway this season. I should be there.

But not only the chance to see the final been taken from me, I've been robbed of the euphoria I was feeling last night after that amazing win. I should still be buzzing now. I should probably still be buzzing this time next week. Instead I feel thoroughly fed up already. Thanks Uefa.

Monday May 5
Newcastle United (away)

I did fancy going to this bank holiday afternoon game, but again I'm in the middle of a run of night shifts. I've only been to St James's Park once, for the final game of the season two years ago. When tickets went on sale it looked like it could be the title decider so I bought one straight away. Then we clinched the league in that wonderful 3-0 win over United and by the time we went to Newcastle the foot was well off the gas. So I got to see a virtual reserve team in action – Jimmy Smith and Lenny Pidgeley played – and we lost 1-0 through a Titus Bramble volley (yes, really). The train fare was close to £100 and I was gutted as I realised from his prolonged wave to the crowd at the end that William Gallas was leaving. It's not a day I look back on fondly. I feel like I went to Newcastle by mistake.

Today I prise myself out of bed in time to watch it in Fortress Living Room. Man United's unsurprisingly comfortable 4-1 win over West Ham on Saturday (a few days after Alan Curbishley said it would be a travesty if United didn't win the league and he would raise a glass if they did) means we have to beat Newcastle to pull level on points at the top again. And we haven't won up there since December 2001.

I can't help thinking the ideal way for Kevin Keegan to finally get revenge on Ferguson for that "I'd love it if we beat them" season would be to let us win 25-0 today, giving us an unbeatable goal difference advantage over the Mancs. But apparently results like that get investigated these days.

Terry clears a Michael Owen shot off the line and then heads against the bar himself. But on the hour Drogba swings over a great free-kick on to Ballack's head and it's 1-0. The same brilliant combination that put us in front against United.

Newcastle hit back well – they've been in good form and are unbeaten in seven – but we weather the storm and keep them out. And with eight minutes left a sweet passing move ends with Malouda slotting the ball into the corner of the net. It's his first goal since we played Schalke in October and his first in the league since the opening day. He's been a big disappointment but played well today.

2-0 and it goes to the final day. We're level on points with Man United but their goal difference is 17 better than ours, so we need Wigan to take something off them next Sunday and us to beat Bolton. That's the Wigan managed by United legend Steve Bruce.

The last time the top two went into the final day level on points was 40 years ago, with the fixtures on the very same date as this year's final day – May 11. Manchester United, who had just qualified for the European Cup final, started the day ahead of a team in blue (Manchester City) on goal difference, but blew it by not winning. Omen? Sounds like one. Let's forget they went on to win that final...

Thursday May 8

Tickets for the Champions League final are now on sale to all season ticket holders and members. It shows they're struggling to shift them – as you'd expect by the vast numbers who aren't going. It means people who've never been to a game in their lives but paid the £30-odd membership fee at the start of the season could be at the final cheering on 'their' team. What a mess this has become.

Joe Cole is voted player of the year. I voted for Ricardo Carvalho, but Joe would have been my second choice. It's been a difficult year to pick one out, largely because so many of our best players have been out so much of the season. Drogba's missed 19 league games – exactly half the season – while Terry has missed 15, Lampard 14, Cech 12 and Essien 11. Ricky himself has only played in 21 league games, while Michael Ballack, our best player in the second half of the season, only played his first game on December 19 and has missed 20 league matches. The fact we're still in with a shout of winning the league despite that many brilliant players out for so many games says an awful lot for the strength of our squad.

Sunday May 11
Bolton (home)

Here we are then. The day the title will be decided. Despite the fact we're possibly 90 minutes away from winning the league, I haven't been feeling that excited over the past few days. For us to finish top we have to better United's result, and I fully expect them to beat Wigan. When Wigan took a point off us, their reaction was more along the lines of "Man United will be pleased!" than any pride in their own achievement, and ever since then I've not been expecting much. But we shouldn't have to be relying on anyone else.

If I haven't been all that excited and nervous this week, today it starts. I find myself thinking "What if??" and on the way down it hits me – we could be watching John Terry lift the Premiership trophy in a few hours. The very thought seems incredible given the state we were in when Jose left.

It's another glorious summer's day, as the final day of the season should be. The stadium is bathed in sunshine, there's not a coat in sight and Big Sam is wearing shorts.

Ricky is absent – he went off injured against Newcastle and hasn't recovered. That's the 17th league game he's missed this season. Alex has been a fantastic stand-in and it's a good job he has been. It's not often your third choice centre-back plays more matches than either of the two men who should be blocking his path to the first team, but that's happened this year.

Bolton are as good as safe, but not mathematically certain. If we beat them 5-0, Fulham win at Portsmouth and Reading win 6-0 at Derby, Bolton will be down. It sounds unlikely, but I've seen Derby play and there's nothing to suggest they wouldn't fulfil their end of the bargain.

Bolton need a point to be certain of staying up. And it looks like they've come for one. They play with El-Hadji Diouf on the halfway line and 10 behind the ball, usually around the edge of the penalty area. They'll be hard to break down.

The team are wearing next season's shirt, which went on sale this week. I haven't bought mine yet, because I want to see which players are still going to be here come August before I get anyone's name put on the back. I want Carvalho on there but not if he's playing for Real Madrid. The new keeper's shirt is bright orange and a few minutes into the game Dan, Mark and I begin counting how many we can see in the crowd. They stand out so brightly we can see at least four in the West Stand, three in the East Stand Upper Tier and a couple in the Shed End. They make the fluorescent yellow away kit look like a funeral outfit.

But while we're counting the glowing attire, John Terry goes up for a ball with Cech and Kevin Davies and lands in a crumpled heap. He's not a man to stay down injured unless something really is up and when a stretcher comes out we know it's bad. As he leaves the pitch to enormous applause my Chelsea-supporting friend Sarah texts me to say it looks like a broken arm. If that's correct, he'll miss the Champions League final. What awful timing for him and the team.

It leaves the atmosphere subdued for a while but things liven up when a huge cheer from the West Stand leads us to believe Wigan have gone in front. It takes a few minutes to discover they haven't. Is someone in the West Stand having a laugh, or is somebody the victim of a cruel friend texting them wrong information? The confusion could be removed by the scores from the other matches being on the scoreboard like they are for every other game but, today of all days, they've decided not to bother with that.

News soon comes through that United have taken the lead through a penalty. Sarah confirms it, so I know this one is true. We reach half-time goalless and although it would only take a goal from us and a Wigan equaliser to turn it round, I feel like the challenge has come to an end.

Dan Petrescu is on the pitch at half-time and gets a fantastic reception. So he should, he was a wonderful player for us. Graeme Le Saux is also on duty, drawing a raffle for a holiday in Abu Dhabi. I don't win. He was another exceptional player and I wish they were both playing today.

After the break we hit the bar and then on the hour mark we get three corners in a row. From the third a Lampard shot falls into the path of substitute Shevchenko, who prods it home. He might have lost his pace but he's still a born goalscorer and I wish we'd made more use of him in recent weeks. He's got eight goals in 25 games this season, compared with Anelka's two in 23.

We've done our bit and now we're just waiting for Wigan to do theirs. Yeah, right. Giggs puts United 2-0 up and it's all over. In the third minute of injury time Bolton get a corner, we make a hash of dealing with it and Matt Taylor sticks it through Cech's legs for 1-1. There's hardly time to restart before the final whistle goes.

A lot of people are gutted by this equaliser, for various reasons. There's the obvious one of wanting to win rather than draw in any match, while others are disappointed we won't finish level on points with United. But to be honest it doesn't really matter. We still finish second. A proud, impressive second, unbeaten since Christmas and with only one defeat since September and the highest number of points any runners-up have ever had, but second nonetheless.

The players come out for a 'lap of appreciation'. John Terry leads them out, which is encouraging, though he doesn't look comfortable and has his arm in a sling. It's a dislocated elbow, not a break and he says he hopes to be okay for Moscow. If he is, and it's not just him talking fearlessly as usual, that's great news.

As the players come round the pitch, accompanied by many of their children, I try to work out who looks like they're saying goodbye. I think quite a few could be going, especially if Mourinho comes calling from Italy. I doubt Drogba will be back and I'm sure Jose would love to sign Lampard and Carvalho too. Until recently I thought Lampard might go in the summer, but after everything he's been through in the past few weeks I think now he might stay, to be close to his dad, and for a bit of familiarity in his life. I hope so. He would be a huge loss.

But the players won't feel like they are saying goodbye, even if they won't be back at the Bridge. They still have one more game, in Moscow, and they probably think they'll be seeing us all there. The fact hardly any of us real fans are going may not have filtered through to them.

The players get a great reception, as does Avram Grant. He walks along behind the players, shaking hands with many people at the front of the crowd and being hugged by plenty too. I'm happy to join in with a rousing round of applause for him as he passes us. He's taken some terrible stick, some of it from me, but has remained dignified and has, let's not forget, helped us to second in the league and the Champions League final. Not bad. Still nobody sings his name though. His children come running across the pitch to him and they embrace each other on the touchline. It's quite a moving moment.

Malouda's son and three daughters perform their own lap of honour-style run along the edge of the pitch in front of us, waving to all and sundry. It's hilarious and, frankly, better than anything their dad has managed all season.

Everybody drifts away one by one and it's the first time in the five years I've had a season ticket that a few of us haven't been for a beer together after the final home game.

Wednesday May 21
Manchester United (Champions League final, Moscow)

Admit it. You expected me to pitch up in Moscow didn't you? It's a book after all – it had to have some sort of dramatic happy ending, eh? I'd look online and find an obscure Eastern European airline flying from Stornoway to St Petersburg for fifty quid. I'd discover a previously-unknown family connection to Maria Sharapova and she'd let me stay in her house. Or maybe Big Sam would reveal himself as a business colleague of Roman and hire a plane for everyone who sits near him to get to the match.

Well, no. Of course it's a book, but it's not a work of fiction. There's no happy ending in terms of getting there, so the best I can hope for is a happy ending on the pitch.

Instead I'll be watching the game in SW6, and that's the next best thing. I catch the coach down to London for the last time this season – I must be National Express's best customer, watch their profits sink during the close season – and head for my hotel round the corner from Earls Court. I've booked a hotel because if we win I don't want to be glancing at my watch and thinking about having to head home.

When I arrive the bloke on reception spots my Chelsea jacket (Umbro late 70s replica style) and says "You're here for the match then? Everybody's here for the match or the Chelsea Flower Show." When I mention not having been able to go to Moscow he looks at me blankly, then says "Oh of course, it's the final isn't it? So many people are staying here I was thinking it was a home game!" Yet another indication of how many fans haven't been able to go.

I make my way towards the ground and a steward tells me the Blue Bar (I thought it was still called the Shed Bar?) is already full and not letting anyone else in. It's about 4.30pm, over three hours until kick-off.

There are hundreds, if not thousands, of fans around already. It's busy in the megastore, there are about 50 people in the road outside the So Bar and many more milling around Fulham Broadway. Tim has booked a table in TGI Fridays. While waiting for him and Mark I peer through the window. It's got several screens and there aren't many people in there. It looks like it could be a masterstroke. Mark arrives and we pop quickly into the Slug, where a friend of his has positioned himself near the ladies toilets for a good view of the totty going past. The pub is packed already.

Tim arrives and we head into TGI's. I've never been here before and am amazed to see it's the old entrance to the tube station. The ticket windows and 'TRAINS THIS WAY' sign have been adapted into features of the restaurant. It seems appropriate, bringing back memories of standing in this very concourse during the post-1997 FA Cup final festivities, chatting to an amiable copper who'd been encouraging revellers to get off the roof. He said he was too embarrassed to admit which "sad" team he supported, before eventually revealing it was Spurs.

Dan has disappointingly chosen to watch the game in Redhill, but Tony arrives, as do Mark's girlfriend Anna, his mates Charlie and Paul and a friend of Tim's called Cliff. Amanda, who sits in the row behind us and always wears a mad self-constructed hat, a furry Russian effort festooned with Chelsea pictures, is here. It's the first time I've ever spoken to her. She calls it her "magic hat". If it helps us win tonight, I'll happily accept it has the powers of Paul Daniels and David Blane combined.

Ashley Cole got clobbered by a Makelele tackle in training yesterday, but he's fit. Essien is at right back and Malouda's reward for a season of huge under-achievement and failure to look remotely interested is a starting place in the Champions League final in place of Kalou. The rest of the team picks itself.

Our food arrives almost exactly on kick-off, which is not ideal, but through my vegetable fajitas I can see United playing the better football. And in the 26th minute, my plate by now long empty, they go in front. A cross from the right by Wes Brown finds Ronaldo, who has escaped his marker Essien, and he heads perfectly into the net. It's so close to the post Cech doesn't even dive. Most at fault, sadly, is Essien. He's a midfielder being asked to play in defence and Ferguson has exploited this by playing Ronaldo on his flank instead of Cole's. And he lost his man, leaving the Portuguese twat to score his first-ever goal against us, following Rooney's last month.

As the half moves on, and the number of empty beer bottles on the table increases rapidly, Ballack has our best chance so far but Van Der Sar makes a good save. But better opportunities fall to United and Cech makes an amazing double save to stop them increasing the lead. This is breathtaking stuff.

And then, right on half-time, Essien's speculative shot takes a couple of deflections off defenders and falls perfectly for Lampard, who is doing what nobody in the world does as well as him – sniffing around for a chance on the edge of the box. He buries it. 1-1! We all leap out of our seats. I run around like a lunatic and then hug various people. Mark runs over to celebrate with the fans who are watching through the window, faces pressed up against the glass like Dickensian paupers drooling outside a lavish banquet.

The replays show Frank pointing to the sky and saying "That's for you" as he celebrates. He's a credit to his mum.

I phone dad at half-time and we agree we're happy to be level after that half. But level we are. My phone is busy with texts from all manner of people, Chelsea and otherwise. I'm touched by how many people want us to win.

In the second half we're by far the better team, have more of the ball and far more shots than United. But the closest we come to taking the lead is a fantastic curling shot by Drogba that rebounds off the post. So it's extra time.

We continue playing well and Lampard hits the bar with a sublime chip on the turn. Two shots off the woodwork, how close can you get? But United have a great chance too. A Ryan Giggs shot beats Cech but Terry heads it clear brilliantly. Then, with four minutes to go and penalties looming, a stupid melee sparked by Tevez and involving most players ends with a red card for Drogba. Replays show he gave Vidic a really timid slap. What a stupid thing to do. Is it his last action in a Chelsea shirt? Who knows, but we do know he can't take a penalty.

When the shoot-out comes a few of us stand in line with our arms around each other, like the players. I don't know why, we just do. Tevez scores. Ballack scores – of course. Carrick scores. Belletti – on as a last minute sub obviously to take a pen, chosen ahead of Sheva – scores. Then, Cech saves Ronaldo's penalty. We go berserk again. Mark leaps up and accidentally headbutts me but I don't care. Of all the people to miss it's the arrogant show pony! We calm down in time to see Lampard score, what a hero, and we're in front. Hargreaves scores, then Ashley Cole scores. If Nani misses we've won. But he doesn't. But now if Terry scores we've won. Van Der Sar goes the wrong way, but it clips the outside of the post. Unbelievable. He slipped and fell as he took it. No-one deserves such bad luck, least of all him.

The effect on the atmosphere is tangible. We were seconds from winning, now it's sudden death and United have had such a let-off. Anderson scores. Kalou scores. Giggs scores. Anelka has his shot saved. It's over.

Silence falls upon the restaurant. I feel numb. We all stand around in disbelief. A few of us summon up the courage to carry on watching, others can't. On the screen Terry is in tears, inconsolable. He didn't deserve that. If only Drogba had stayed on. Time seems to stand still for a while. I'm sure we stayed for a few minutes, but (writing this two days later) I can't remember what was happening.

Nobody wants to hang around. If we'd won we'd have been partying in the street for hours but instead we pay the bill and everyone says their goodbyes and disappears into the night.

I trudge slowly back to my hotel, totally deflated. What a way for the season to end.

Thursday May 22
Dreams (shattered)

I check out of my hotel. It's a glorious sunny day and I decide to walk across London to Marylebone to get my train. I'm in a foul mood. I walk through Kensington and across Hyde Park with a permanent scowl on my face, my iPod blocking out all the sounds of a world where Manchester Bastard United are European champions.

I buy a copy of the Times because, in a bid to ease the pain, I want to read whatever positive words they can manage about Chelsea. Various writers are charitable to John Terry, saying he didn't deserve it. Of course he didn't. He had the guts to take a penalty, a captain leading by example. His reward was to end the night in tears. In contrast United's skipper Rio Ferdinand hid in the background, not taking any of their seven penalties, and he got to lift the trophy. There's no justice.

The papers – my need for more kind words leads to the Sun and Standard – are similarly generous to Lampard and Grant. The words of ire are saved for Drogba, his stupid sending-off clearly seen as a summing-up of his time at the club. It's harsh on the man who scored 33 goals last season, won the Golden Boot, was runner-up for Player of the Year, was in the top three of World Player of the Year and has scored for us in four cup finals, but this will be what he's remembered for. His legacy is diving, moaning and petulance, a red card on the biggest stage.

I'm reading the papers while having a coffee at Speaker's Corner. A German family are sat on the bench next to me. The daughter, who must be about 11 or 12, comes over and asks "Can I please make a photo with you, so I can win five Euros?" I nod in bemused agreement and her mother takes a snap of us both. I can barely summon up the energy to look up and I'm certainly not smiling. Christ knows how she's winning five Euros. It must be a school project to be photographed with the most miserable bastard in a European capital. If so, she's a shoe-in.

I head back to Birmingham.

Saturday May 24

At 6pm Chelsea announce Avram Grant has been sacked. It's hardly a surprise. Reports suggest he was offered his old director of football role but turned it down. No doubt tomorrow's papers will say we've treated a dignified man badly, lack class, have rewarded a man who nearly won us three trophies with the sack, and so on.

But the truth is Grant was never the right man for the job. The football was supposed to improve under him and it hasn't. He was found tactically and inspirationally wanting at some vital moments, most obviously the Carling Cup final. And while he's behaved with dignity lately, let's not forget he turned up at the club last summer against Mourinho's wishes and within a couple of months Jose had gone – Grant had his job. He may have had nothing to do with Jose going, but maybe he did. I guess we'll never know, but there are many fans who regard him as a back-stabber for his possible role in Mourinho's departure.

I wouldn't say I'm delighted he's gone. We've come close to some big trophies and if the club had decided to give him another season I'd have accepted it. But if he's replaced by a manager with more experience at a big club and a proven record of success, then it will be a good move. I'm not entirely convinced how much of this decent but ultimately fruitless season (we're the first English club ever to be runners-up in three competitions in one year) has been down to the manager anyway. I may be doing him a disservice, but I think the players have probably carried the team along largely on their own – especially the dressing room leaders and particularly John Terry.

So who will be the next manager? Frank Rijkaard is available, having left Barcelona, and I think he'd be ideal. He had great success at Barcelona playing lovely football and is a manager top players will want to play for. What more can you ask for? Guus Hiddink is an old mate of Roman's and may be available after Russia depart Euro 2008. Mark Hughes is a Chelsea old boy who's done a great job at Blackburn. There's a part of me that would love to see Ruud Gullit back, despite him doing very little in the decade he's been gone.

And the back page story in today's Sun is all about Roman and Jose becoming pals again and speaking several times lately. How bizarre would it be if the Special One came back? I can't see it happening, but I'd love it if it did. That really would be special.

Chapter 11

Phil us up

Wednesday June 11

When I set out to keep a diary of the season, I didn't expect any June entries. I expected the season to finish in May, probably with Jose Mourinho lifting another trophy or two for us.

I didn't expect to be writing about the successor to Jose's successor. It's a funny old game.

But this evening the next man in the warmest of hotseats was unveiled. I was sitting at work, one eye on the computer and one eye on Switzerland v Turkey in the European Championships, when the news came through. It's Big Phil – Luis Felipe Scolari, the Portugal manager.

I'll be honest, he wouldn't have been my first choice, but that's not to say I'm disappointed. His teams play nice football, he's a big character, the sort of manager who'll attract good players and he's successful. He's won the World Cup, how many managers can say that?

Scolari previously said he wasn't going to decide anything until the Euros were over, but this announcement comes right in the middle of the first week of the tournament, the day after Portugal's second win out of two. I expect Chelsea wanted to announce it to attract decent new players as soon as possible and to prevent some of the best of our current crop heading off into the arms of the new Inter manager, one Jose Mourinho. Ricardo Carvalho said this week he fancied playing for Jose again, now he's saying how much he loves playing for Big Phil.

There are two months until next season starts. I daresay we'll have a lot of new faces by then. Brazilians? Some of the stars of the Portugal team? Sounds exciting. I doubt we'll see Drogba again. There are a few we wouldn't miss, such as Sidwell, Wright-Phillips and Boulahrouz, and there are some who've been disappointments and might look to move on, including Malouda and Anelka. Makelele and Sheva aren't getting any younger and Carlo deserves to be someone's first choice keeper. I hope the likes of Lampard, Essien, Carvalho and Cech don't decide they still want to be back with Jose – Big Phil or no Big Phil.

One thing's for sure. I'll still be there and so will 40-odd thousand others, including all my near-neighbours in the Matthew Harding lower tier. We'll be there through rain or shine, wins and defeats, cup finals, penalty shoot-outs, management changes, defeats to Barnsley and unexpected trips to brothels in Athens. Because that's what you do when you're a football fan. You don't leave, you don't move on and you don't get transferred. You're always there, you're always involved and you always care what happens. Here's to being part of Big Phil's Blue Army.

It's going to be fun.

Also available from Heroes Publishing

HUNDRED WATTS
a life in music
by RON WATTS

With Foreword by former Sex Pistol
Glen Matlock

Ron Watts remains one of the most influential men in
the history of British music.
From John Lee Hooker to Johnny Rotten, Bowie to Bono,
Ron got to know and work with the biggest and the best.
From bringing Blues greats to Britain, to his central role
in the 1976 Punk Festival at London's legendary 100 Club,
he helped shape youth culture in the UK.
Hundred Watts is the informative, revealing and extremely
funny account of his days at the cutting edge
of the music business.
Price – £7.99
ISBN – 0954388445

Also available from Heroes Publishing

IT'LL BE DIFFERENT NEXT YEAR
more life in the Football League
by STEVE PHELPS

When Coventry City supporter Steve Phelps began recording
the 2007-08 season, he didn't have any idea of how the
following months would turn out. Early hopes of promotion
back to the Promised Land of the Premier League – and a
memorably easy cup win at Old Trafford – gave way to a
speedy descent of the table as teams who had previously just
been names on the pools coupon took advantage
of the Sky Blues' on-field largesse.
Add the threat of administration, the welcome appearance of a
knight in shining armour and the annual sacking of the
manager and you have another chapter in the unpredictable
history of Coventry City FC. But as Steve says –
It'll be different next year.

Price – £5.99
ISBN 0954388488 – EAN 9780954388485

HEROES PUBLISHING
PO Box 1703, Perry Barr, Birmingham, B42 1UZ
www.heroespublishing.com